V-FORCE
Britain's Airborne
Nuclear Deterrent

V-FORCE

Britain's Airborne Nuclear Deterrent

Robert Jackson

Ian Allan PUBLISHING

Front Cover:
Vulcans on an operational take-off at Scampton. *MoD*

Back Cover, Top:
A Victor B2 of No 100 Squadron armed with a Blue Steel stand-off missile.
MoD (RAF)

Back Cover, Bottom:
A Valiant B(K)1 pictured over southern England in the late 1950's.
MoD (RAF)

Half Title Page:
Valiant B(K)1s. *MoD (RAF)*

Title Page:
Avro Vulcan B2. *MoD (RAF)*

Below:
A Victor K2 of the Marham Tanker Wing refuelling a Phantom. *MoD (RAF)*

First published 2000

ISBN 0 7110 2750 1

© Robert Jackson 2000

Published by Ian Allan Publishing

an imprint of Ian Allan Publishing Ltd, Terminal House, Shepperton, Surrey TW17 8AS.

Printed by Ian Allan Printing Ltd, Riverdene Business Park, Hersham, Surrey KT12 4RG.

Code: 0003/B

CONTENTS

Glossary		6
Introduction		8
1	Britain's Bomb: Conception of the Deterrent	14
2	Soviet Strategic Forces 1945-55	22
3	Britain's Deterrent: Valiant Days	30
4	Britain's Deterrent: The Blue Streak IRBM	48
5	Valiant Combat: Suez, 1956	51
6	Enter the Vulcan and Victor	57
7	The 'Grapple' Trials	68
8	Shaping the Force: Alerts and Exercises	71
9	Defending the V-Bomber Bases	83
10	Bomber Command's Thor Missiles	87
11	The Mk 2 V-Bombers and Stand-off Weapons	92
12	V-Force Support: Reconnaissance and Countermeasures	105
13	V-Force Operations, 1963-8	113
14	Conventional Strike Force	129
15	V-Force Support: The Tanker Forces	139
Appendices		
1	The V-Force Squadrons	149
2	The Soviet Union: Potential Targets	155
Notes		156
Index		158

GLOSSARY

ADD	Soviet Long-Range Aviation Force
AEO	Air electronics officer
AFB	Air force base
AFMED	Allied Forces Mediterranean
Airborne Cigar	Jamming transmitter
AMC	USAF Air Materiel Command
AOC-in-C	Air Officer Commander-in-Chief
ASI	Air speed indicator
AWRE	Air Weapons Research establishment
BG	Bomber Group
Black Knight	Blue Streak re-entry test vehicle
Blue Danube	The first British atomic weapon
Blue Rapier	Missile designed by Bristol
Blue Streak	British IRBM
BS	Bombardment Squadron
C of A	Controller of Aircraft
CENTO	Central Treaty Organisation
COMASWFORLANT	Commander, Antisubmarine Warfare Force, Atlantic
DA	Dal'naya Aviatsiya
DEFCON	Defense Condition
ECM	Electronic countermeasures
ELINT	Electronic intelligence
Exercise 'Jungle King'	Simulated attack on US airfields at Fürstenfeldbruck and Rhein-Main, March 1953
Exercise 'Kinsman'	Squadron dispersal exercise
Exercise 'Mayflight'	Exercise in which all aspects of the Bomber Command dispersal and readiness plan were practised
Exercise 'Micky Finn'	A no-notice dispersal exercise that could happen at any time of day or night
Exercise 'Rat/Terrier'	Low-level test attacks on USAF bases at Lakenheath and Sculthorpe to test the defences, May 1953
Exercise 'Rejuvenate'	To give Fighter Command aircraft interception practice in the sector covering the northwest approaches to the UK
Exercise 'Skyshield'	October 1961, designed to test the efficiency of NORAD
Exercise 'Vigilant'	May 1957. No 543 Squadron conducted night radar targeting raids

Flt Lt	Flight Lieutenant
GCI	Ground-Controlled Interception
GEN75	The committee of British senior ministers
GH (p51) or GeeH	Radar navigational aid
GMT	Greenwich mean time
Gp Capt	Group Captain
Green Bamboo	The assembly under development for a free-falling megaton weapon and air-launched missile
Green Granite	Nuclear warhead test assembly
HER	High Explosive Research
ICBM	Intercontinental ballistic missile
IFF	Identification Friend/Foe
Indigo Hammer	A 6kt plutonium nuclear warhead device for Bloodhound
Indigo Violet	Bloodhound's guidance system
INS	Inertial navigation system
IOC	Initial operational capability
IRBM	Intermediate-range ballistic missile
ITP	Instruction to proceed
kN	Kilo Newton (SI equivalent of pounds [lb] thrust)
kT	Kiloton
kt	Knots
M	Mach
MC	Medium Capacity
MoS	Ministry of Supply
MRBM	Medium-range ballistic missile
mT	Megaton
NBS	Navigation and bombing system
NEAF	Near East Air Force
nm	Nautical miles
NORAD	North American Air Defense Command
OCU	Operational Conversion Unit
Operation 'Antler' at	The series of British nuclear tests the Maralinga Range, South Australia, August 1957
Operation 'Black Buck'	Vulcan missions flown against Argentine installations on the Falklands
Operation 'Corporate'	The Falklands operation
Operation 'Crossroads'	Atomic testing on Bikini Atoll

Operation 'Pontifex'	Aerial survey of Northern and Southern Rhodesia and Bechuanaland
OR (1001)	Operational Requirement (1001)
Orange Herald	Blue Streak megaton warhead assembly
ORB	Operations Record Book
Project 'E'	The supply of US nuclear weapons to the RAF
Purple Granite	Warhead
QRA	Quick Reaction Alert
R&D	Research and development
RAE	Royal Aircraft Establishment
Red Beard	British free-fall nuclear weapon
Red Rapier	Missile designed by Vickers
Red Snow	Megaton range warhead fitted to Blue Steel
'Red Steer'	British tail warning radar
rpm	Revs per minute
SAC	USAF's Strategic Air Command

SAM	Surface-to-air missile
Short Granite	Nuclear warhead
SLBM	Submarine-launched ballistic missile
SM	Strategic missile
SMS	Strategic Missile Squadron
Sqn Ldr	Squadron Leader
SRS	Strategic Reconnaissance Squadron
st	Static thrust
TERCOM	Terrain contour matching
SAC	Strategic Air Command
TIR	Target illuminating radar
U235	Uranium 235
Violet Club	Interim high-yield weapon
Wg Cdr	Wing Commander
Yellow Aster	Code-name for the H2S Mk 9, a non-scanning radar system designed to carry out all-weather reconnaissance operations
Yellow Sun Mk 1 and Mk 2	British free-fall megaton weapon

INTRODUCTION

At 08.15hrs on Monday, 6 August 1945, a single Boeing B-29 Superfortress with the name Enola Gay emblazoned on its nose, droned high over the Japanese city of Hiroshima, in southern Honshu. From its belly fell the first operational atomic bomb, nicknamed 'Little Boy'. Minutes later 4.7 square miles of Hiroshima lay totally destroyed beneath the ascending mushroom cloud. In all, 70,000 people were killed and as many more were injured by blast, heat and radiation. The next day, US President Harry Truman announced to the world:

'Sixteen hours ago an American airplane dropped one bomb on Hiroshima, an important Japanese Army base. That bomb had more power than 20,000 tons of TNT . . . It is an atomic bomb.'

Three days later on the morning of Thursday, 9 August, another B-29 dropped an atomic bomb on Nagasaki. This second nuclear attack, together with the invasion of Japanese-held Manchuria that same day, pushed the Japanese government over the brink to unconditional surrender.

In the final analysis, it was the B-29 strategic bomber that destroyed Japan's capacity for waging war. Although there is no doubt that it was the atomic bomb that brought Japan to the surrender table, it was only the latest in a long series of shattering blows. Japan had been seriously weakened by the terrible losses she had sustained both in the Pacific and Burma, and she was being slowly strangled by the Allied blockade of her communications. Nevertheless, it was the continual battering by the B-29s of the USAAF's 21st Bomber Command, more than any other single cause, that brought her to defeat. The great fire raids on 60 of Japan's cities had a fearful effect on civilian morale, and the dispersal of her aircraft and aero-engine plants under conditions of panic caused as much dislocation of production as did the raids themselves. In the words of the Japanese premier, Suzuki:

'It seemed to me unavoidable that in the long run Japan would be almost destroyed by air attack, so that merely on the basis of the B-29s alone I was convinced that Japan should sue for peace. On top of the B-29 raids came the atomic bombs, after the Potsdam Declaration, which was just one additional reason for giving in. I myself, on the basis of the B-29 raids, felt that the cause was hopeless.'

At no other time in the history of air warfare had the strategic bomber succeeded so overwhelmingly in its task. Strategic air warfare had defeated a deadly enemy, and had laid waste his capacity to fight. It had become a weapon of awesome power which, now allied with nuclear force, could be a destroyer of nations — or a preserver of peace.

So the concept of nuclear deterrence was born, bringing with it an awesome responsibility for the nations that came to base their strategic policies upon it. Foremost among them was the United States, and the arm of its forces that would bear the responsibility: the United States Air Force Strategic Air Command (SAC).

The primary mission of what was to become the mightiest war machine the world had ever seen was defined in simple enough terms. The new command had to:

'. . . be prepared to conduct long range offensive operations in any part of the world either independently or in

Left and Far Left:
Hiroshima, 6 August 1945. From this moment on, the world would live under the shadow of the atomic bomb. *Author's Collection*

co-operation with land and naval forces; to conduct maximum range reconnaissance over land or sea either independently or in co-operation with land and naval forces; to provide combat units capable of intense and sustained combat operations employing the latest and most advanced weapons; to train units and personnel for the maintenance of the Strategic Force in all parts of the world; to perform such special missions as the Commanding General, Army Air Forces may direct.' [1]

Yet, when SAC came into existence on 21 March 1946, its material assets were slender and were to become even more so before the political climate of the late 1940s dictated rapid expansion and re-equipment. The formation of the new command was simple enough on paper; it was achieved by the expedient of redesignating Headquarters Continental Air Forces as Headquarters Strategic Air Command. SAC HQ was established at Bolling Field, Washington DC, and was allocated the whole of the US Second Air Force, whose HQ was located at Colorado Springs. The command was concentrated on 22 major bases and also controlled over 30 minor ones; personnel strength was about 100,000. SAC's commanding general was Gen George C. Kenney, but as he was at that time the senior US representative on the Military Staff Committee of the United Nations, his deputy, Maj-Gen St Clair Streett, served as SAC's commanding general until Kenney could assume full responsibility in October 1946. Brig-Gen Frederic H. Smith, Jr, was Chief of Staff.

By this time, SAC HQ had moved from Bolling to Andrews Field, Maryland. The command's offensive strength now comprised nine very heavy bomb groups, all equipped with Boeing B-29s and each with a paper establishment of 30 aircraft. In fact only six of the groups had been assigned aircraft, and even then they were under strength, the total number of B-29s on SAC's inventory in the autumn of 1946 standing at 148. The Command was still a conventional bombing force; only one unit, the 509th Bomber Group (BG) — the group formed specifically for dropping the first operational atomic bombs — had aircraft that were suitably modified to carry these large, bulky, first-generation nuclear weapons. (As a point of interest, the equipment used to hoist the early atomic bombs into the B-29s was of British design, the type used to load six-ton 'Tallboy' and 10-ton 'Grand Slam' bombs into the RAF's Lancasters.)

In July 1946, the 509th BG took part in Operation 'Crossroads'. Centred on Bikini Atoll, the object of this exercise was to study the effects of two nuclear explosions on a simulated naval force consisting of captured and time-expired warships. The exercise involved the efforts of some 42,000 personnel, operating under a provisional organisation known as Task Force One. Task Group 1.5, the Army Air Force contingent, consisted of about 2,200 personnel drawn mainly from SAC and commanded by Brig-Gen Roger M. Ramey, officer commanding the 58th Bombardment Wing. Task Group 1.5 was responsible for delivering the air-

dropped atomic bomb (the other, a device rather than a bomb, was to be attached to a ship and exploded under water) and for providing aircraft to photograph the explosion and collect scientific data.

On 1 July 1946, Dave's Dream, a 509th BG B-29 piloted by Major Woodrow P. Swancutt and temporarily based on the island of Kwajalein, dropped a Nagasaki-type (plutonium) bomb on 73 ships assembled off Bikini. The air-bursting weapon, of about 18kT yield, destroyed five of the ships and severely damaged nine others. Task Group 1.5 also took part in the second phase of Operation 'Crossroads', the underwater explosion of 25 July, by providing aircraft for photographic, data collection and support functions.

In October 1946, in accordance with its stated global role, SAC dispatched an entire B-29 group outside the limits of the

Above:
The Boeing B-29 Superfortress was the most advanced piston-engined bomber of World War 2, and was the mainstay of Strategic Air Command in the immediate postwar years. *Author's Collection*

continental United States for the first time on a period of temporary duty. The 28th BG deployed from Grand Island Army Air Field, Nebraska, to Elmendorf in Alaska for six months of combat training in Arctic conditions, returning in April 1947 to a new base at Rapid City, South Dakota.

Meanwhile, in November 1946, SAC had dispatched aircraft overseas in what was to be the first of many shows of force. The decision to do so came in the wake of the shooting down of two US Army C-47s over Yugoslavia by Soviet fighter aircraft. Col James C. Selser, Jr, commanding the 43rd BG at Davis-Monthan Field, Arizona, led a flight of six B-29s to Rhein-Main airfield in Germany; they remained there for two weeks, during which time they made several flights along the border of Soviet-occupied territory, visited a number of European locations and surveyed several airfields for possible

future use by SAC B-29s. Quite apart from the operational value of this deployment, it served clear notice on the Soviet Union, at a time of deteriorating East-West relations, that the United States would come to the aid of Western Europe in the event of Soviet aggression.

Meanwhile, in Britain, the awesome power of atomic weapons, and their value as a political as well as a military tool, had not been ignored. Momentous decisions had already been made which, in the fullness of time, would transform the United Kingdom into a leading player on the nuclear stage.

Opposite Page and Above:
Victor K2 tankers of No 55 Squadron pictured on a Middle East deployment to Muharraq for an air exercise. *John Hardy*

Below:
A Vulcan B2, unit unidentified, on a 'lone ranger' sortie to Muharraq. *John Hardy*

1 BRITAIN'S BOMB:
Conception of the Deterrent

At the outset of World War 2 in 1939, Great Britain, alone among the major powers, possessed a bomber force that could truly be described as strategic. Such a force had, in fact, been in existence since the summer of 1918, when a strategic bombing element — known as the Independent Force, RAF — had been formed under the command of Maj-Gen Sir Hugh Trenchard to carry out attacks by day and night against industrial targets, railway centres and aerodromes in Germany. It was the first time that an air force had been formed for the express purpose of conducting a war without reference or subordination to either army or navy.

Small though RAF Bomber Command's strategic force was in 1939, it nevertheless provided the anvil on which a mighty sword was forged: the striking force of four-engined heavy bombers which, from the summer of 1942, began to attack Germany's industrial heartland with growing power. In that year, too, the United States entered the strategic bombing war, with the arrival in Britain of the first units of the USAAF Eighth Air Force; but for the Americans the strategic bomber was a relatively new concept, their land-based air power having been assigned to the role of army support. The same was true of the air arms of both Germany and the USSR, neither of which succeeded in creating a significant strategic bombing force during World War 2. The Japanese, on the other hand, followed Britain's lead by creating a significant strategic bombing arm, which mostly came under the umbrella of the Imperial Japanese Navy and was used to good effect in the Sino-Japanese Manchurian campaign and, later, in Japan's offensives in South-East Asia.

By the war's end, the United States had taken over the lead in strategic bomber design. Whereas the RAF's requirements had called for a bomber capable of delivering a heavy bomb load over medium ranges, resulting in the Short Stirling, Avro Lancaster and Handley Page Halifax, the USAAF's requirement had been different, mainly because of geographical considerations. In the late 1930s, with Imperial Japan posing an increasing threat to American interests in the Pacific, several US aircraft companies were asked to submit design studies for a new and advanced bomber capable of carrying a substantial bomb load over great distances; one which, in other words, would be able to strike at Japan from forward US bases in the Pacific. The result was the Boeing B-29, the strategic bomber that would ultimately project US air power into the atomic age.

In wartime Britain, the emphasis was on developing existing bomber designs to their limit, rather than on seeking new and revolutionary breakthroughs. This trend was personified by the Avro Lincoln, which was developed to Specification B14/43 to meet the need for a Lancaster replacement. It flew for the first time in 1944 and entered service with RAF Bomber Command in 1945, too late to see action in the war. It was to remain the mainstay of Bomber Command until the early 1950s, when it began to be replaced by a jet — the English Electric Canberra light bomber.

It was not until November 1944, with war still raging in Europe and the Far East, that the British Chiefs of Staff asked their Technical Warfare Committee to look ahead and advise them on future weapons and methods of warfare. This committee set up a sub-committee composed of distinguished scientists, headed by Sir Henry Tizard, and asked them to make a report. This became available in July 1945, the month in which the first American atomic device was exploded. Among other things, the report predicted the devastating effects of nuclear weapons and envisaged the development of jet bombers able to cruise at 500mph (800km/h) at 40,000ft (12,200m) carrying a 10,000lb (4,530kg) bomb load. It also contained an important statement:

'The only answer we can see to the atomic bomb is to be prepared to use it ourselves in retaliation. The knowledge that we were prepared, in the last resort, to do this might well deter an aggressive nation.'

So, for the first time, the idea of nuclear deterrence was postulated as a written statement.[2]

After the second American atomic bomb was dropped on Japan in August 1945, the British government — now a Labour administration, returned to power in the General Election of July — appointed a committee of senior ministers to formulate and oversee a policy on atomic energy, Prime Minister Clement Attlee emphasising that a decision on 'policy with regard to the atomic bomb' was imperative. He further told his senior ministers that 'The answer to an atomic bomb on London is an atomic bomb on another great city,' so making it clear that he favoured the principle of nuclear retaliation.[3]

The immediate reaction of the Chiefs of Staff to this new political development was to instruct their Technical Warfare Committee to revise the Tizard Report, and in October 1945 they expressed the view to the Prime Minister that, if the United Nations Organisation (which was inaugurated on 24 October) failed to secure agreement on international atomic energy control, the possession of atomic weapons would be vital to Britain's security. The Chiefs of Staff also accepted the conclusions of the revised Tizard Report, one of which was that, for the next 10 years, the only 'practicable' means of delivering atomic weapons would be by manned bombers. Again, the policy of nuclear deterrence was underpinned in the view of the Chiefs of Staff that:

'The best method of defence against the new weapon is likely to be the deterrent effect that the possession of the means of retaliation would have on a potential aggressor.'[4]

At the end of October 1945, the GEN75 Committee (as the committee of senior ministers was known), armed with the views and opinions of many senior civil and military officials, recommended that the government should undertake the production of atomic bombs as soon as possible. Soon afterwards, in December, another government-appointed body, the Advisory Committee on Atomic Energy, recommended the construction in the United Kingdom of one or two atomic piles for the production of plutonium. This recommendation was endorsed by the Chiefs of Staff, who at the beginning of 1946 urged the Prime Minister that at least two piles should be constructed, cautioning that:

'Until the United Nations Organisation is proved, we require . . . the greatest capacity to make atomic bombs that economic factors and the supply of raw materials will allow'.[5]

The reaction of the GEN75 ministers was to advise that work should proceed on building the first pile, and that a research establishment should be set up at Harwell, then in Berkshire. The Air Ministry had, in fact, listed 17 airfields they were prepared to release for this purpose; Duxford in Cambridgeshire and Debden in Essex were both considered, but the former was rejected because it had a poor water supply, and the latter because it had a high water table. As radioactive waste would be buried on site, a low water table was essential to avoid possible pollution.

At the end of January 1946 the Prime Minister announced the appointment of Professor J. D. Cockcroft as Director of the Harwell Research Establishment; Cockcroft decided to establish his small scientific team in a nearby pub, 'The Horse and Jockey'. At the same time, Marshal of the RAF Lord Portal, who had played such a memorable part as Chief of the Air Staff in World War 2, was appointed Controller of Production of Atomic Energy. In May 1946 Portal visited the United States, and although he was given no access to nuclear energy information (the McMahon Act, which was to become law in the USA in August, forbade the disclosure of US atomic energy information to other states, including Britain), he

returned to the UK determined that Britain should 'think big, take chances and translate into reality the priority which the government have afforded to the atomic energy project.'[6]

During the latter half of 1946 Portal acquired an invaluable assistant in the person of Dr William Penney, who had been involved with the American atomic bomb project and who had been one of two British observers to witness the Nagasaki drop (the other was Gp Capt Leonard Cheshire VC). Penney worked directly under Portal in the Ministry of Supply, and supervised an RAF team under Wg Cdr J. S. Rowlands, whose task it was to supervise the assembly of the first British atomic bomb and eventually see it into service.

The project went ahead disguised under the name of High Explosive Research (HER) and was controlled from the Ministry of Supply establishment at Aldermaston in Berkshire, a former USAAF airfield. The other sites involved in the project were Fort Halstead in Kent, the Armament Research Establishment (ARE) — where Penney and his team worked on their calculations and designs; ARE Woolwich — a sub-station of Fort Halstead where metallurgical work was carried out; the MoS factories at Springfields — the uranium metal factory near Preston in Lancashire; Windscale in Cumberland, where plutonium was produced; and also the Royal Aircraft Establishment at Farnborough, which was responsible for the ballistic design of the bomb case. The only non-government organisation involved was Hunting Engineering Ltd, which was contracted to make the whole of the bomb's centre-section, including the nuclear capsule with its explosive lenses. Hunting did not actually handle any explosives, using inert replicas instead. Aldermaston was responsible for assembling the bombs and delivering them to the RAF.[7]

Active planning for the development of the British atomic bomb — which was named 'Blue Danube' — began in July 1946, following a recommendation to this effect by the Chiefs of Staff, and on 9 August the Air Staff issued Operational Requirement 1001 (OR1001) for a bomb 'employing the principles of nuclear fission'. In mid-December, the Air Staff drafted an Operational Requirement (OR229) for an aircraft capable of carrying the bomb. The aircraft envisaged had to be able to deliver a 10,000lb (4,530kg) store at 500kt (915km/h) to a target 1,500nm (2,780km) away; it was to have a still-air range of 3,500nm (6,485km), with a ceiling of 50,000ft (15,250m) over the target; its bomb load was to be doubled over shorter ranges and was to consist either of conventional weapons or a 'special' (ie nuclear) store accommodated internally.

This meant that the bomb bay would have to house a weapon 25ft (7.63m) in length and 5ft (1.5m) in diameter. The aircraft was to have a five-man crew, accommodated together in a jettisonable pressure cabin; pressure was to be maintained at 9lb/sq in (0.63kg/sq m), equivalent to an altitude of 8,000ft (2,440m), during cruise to the target at 45,000ft (13,725m), reducing to 3.5lb/sq in (0.23kg/sq m) over the target to minimise the risk of explosive decompression if the aircraft sustained damage. The bomber was to be

Left:
The YB-49, Northrop's unsuccessful flying wing jet bomber design. Forty years later, Northrop was to produce the B-2 'stealth' bomber — another flying wing. *Northrop*

Below:
In Britain, too, the flying wing idea was far from new. De Havilland's DH108, first flown on 15 May 1946, was the first British aircraft to exceed the speed of sound. *British Aerospace*

equipped with an advanced version of H2S radar navigational aid for navigation and bombing, but a visual bombing station was also to be provided. Another requirement was that the aircraft was to be capable of being produced in quantity.[8]

The final political decision to develop Britain's own atomic bomb was taken by the GEN75 ministers on 8 January 1947, coincidentally the same day that the Ministry of Supply issued its specification for the first British strategic jet bomber (B35/46) to selected aircraft companies; these were Avro, Armstrong Whitworth, Handley Page, Short Brothers and Vickers-Armstrong. All submitted designs to meet the specification; those of Avro and Handley Page were the ones eventually selected by the Ministry of Supply.

A second specification, B14/46, was issued in August 1947, and was much less demanding than B35/46. It called for an aircraft with the same range, but with a lower ceiling (45,000ft/13,725m) and speed (390kt/720km/h). Using a conventional straight wing design, it was intended as an insurance against delays in fulfilling the more advanced B35/46 specification. It was eventually to materialise in the Short SA4 Sperrin, two prototypes of which were built and used in a variety of trials, including the dropping of 'bomb shapes' connected with the atomic bomb programme.[9]

For Britain's aircraft designers the strategic jet bomber requirement posed a whole new range of problems, not the least of which was that in order to meet the specification fully, aerodynamic design knowledge would have to be pushed to its absolute limits, and perhaps even beyond. Research facilities, too, were greatly inferior to those existing in the United States; throughout the whole industry there was not a single transonic wind tunnel, because, although working examples had been discovered in Germany at the end of the war, these had been dismantled with astonishing speed and shipped back to the USA, along with a vast amount of data on high-speed aerodynamics and design. Nevertheless, the slender amount of German material that remained was to assist the British designers in performing near miracles. All the firms that entered the running to meet B35/46, with the exception of Shorts, were influenced by German data.

A. V. Roe and Company at Chadderton, Manchester, began serious design studies towards meeting the requirements of B35/36 in January 1947. For Roy Chadwick, Avro's technical director, and his design team, the lack of technical information on high-speed flight and configurations, together with the absence of transonic research facilities, meant starting from scratch. First of all, they investigated a series of swept-wing designs, culminating in one with 45 degrees of sweep and swept tail surfaces, but discovered that such an aircraft would be well in excess of the 100,000lb (45,300kg) weight limit imposed by B35/46 and would have a lower performance than that required. They therefore investigated ways to save weight and improve performance, and it seemed that an all-wing design might provide a favourable solution.

The idea was far from new. The Messerschmitt Me163 rocket-propelled fighter had been an all-wing design, with no horizontal tail surfaces, and a lot of research into triangular wing shapes had been carried out in Germany by Dr Alexander Lippisch. The German firm of Horten had also experimented with all-wing aircraft, and the prototype of a fighter, the HoIX, had been nearing completion at the war's end. In Britain, de Havilland had flown the little tailless DH108 in May 1946, while Armstrong Whitworth, after experimenting with all-wing gliders, was building a jet-powered model, the AW52. Chadwick and his team were especially interested in American efforts in the all-wing field, which had produced an experimental four-engined bomber, the Northrop XB-35; this had flown in 1946 and a jet-powered variant was mooted. (This was later to emerge as the YB-49, both prototypes of which exploded in mid-air during the test programme.)[10]

Avro's early ventures into the all-wing design soon showed that they were running into a severe weight penalty. It was clear that the only way in which the weight could be brought within the specification limits was to reduce the aspect ratio substantially without a comparative reduction in wing loading; the result was a wing that was almost a pure triangle, like the Greek letter 'D' — hence the universally adopted name 'Delta'.

The triangular-winged aircraft that Chadwick's team now designed, under the project number Avro 698, was a far cry from what it was later to become in the process of evolution. The crew compartment, housed under a blister canopy, was built into the apex of the triangle; there was no projecting nose section. On either side of the wing's fat centre-section — deep enough for a man to stand upright inside it — two Bristol BE10 engines were to be buried, fed through two large circular air intakes projecting slightly ahead of the wing leading edge. Small, swept fins and rudders were mounted on the wingtips. The bombs were housed in bays situated between the engines and the main undercarriage — or, alternatively, they could be housed on one side only, with the space on the other side filled by extra fuel tanks. The flying controls were based on those fitted to the Armstrong Whitworth AW52 and consisted of double elevons along the wing trailing edge. The design was completed, apart from some minor modifications, by the end of March 1947, and in April it was decided to give the delta project full company backing. Detailed drawings were submitted to the Ministry of Supply in the following month, and the Avro team settled down to await a decision.[11]

Meanwhile, at Cricklewood in north London, the design team of Handley Page had been busily working up its own ideas on the B35/46 theme. Handley Page had been interested in the tailless configuration, having built and flown an experimental aircraft, the Manx, in 1943, and when Chief Designer Reginald S. Stafford went to investigate the achievements of Germany's wartime aircraft industry in June 1945, tailless research data was near the top of his shopping list. Four months later his deputy, Godfrey Lee, also went on an official mission to Germany to study tailless research on

Top Left:
The delta-wing concept used in the design of the Avro Vulcan was tested on small-scale research aircraft, the Avro 707 series. The first Avro 707A, WD280, carried out further work of this type in Australia after 1956. It is now preserved in Melbourne. *British Aerospace*

Bottom Left:
The Avro 707B, seen here, was used for low-speed trials. *British Aerospace*

behalf of the Royal Aircraft Establishment. He took the opportunity to gather much material on the behaviour of various types of swept wing at high Mach numbers, all of which was duly passed on to Handley Page. Most of the German material, in fact, came from the Arado company, which had some very advanced high-speed designs on the drawing board at the war's end. Armed with this new information, the small Handley Page team set about designing a jet-propelled, tailless bomber whose wings had a bold sweep — for that day — of 45 degrees and were tipped by vertical fins and rudders. Flaps were incorporated in the design, so to trim out the pitching movement a tailplane was mounted on a small fin at the mid-point of the wing.

This design, which anticipated B35/46 by several months, was submitted to the Ministry of Aircraft Production in June 1946, and no decision had been made about its future when Handley Page, together with five other companies, was invited to submit a tender to the specification on 1 January 1947. Logically, the design team turned to the tailless bomber design as a basis for further study, but it was soon apparent that a modified wing shape would be necessary if the demands of the specification were to be met. Since neither the delta nor a thin swept wing seemed to offer the ideal solution, Handley Page decided to combine the two, designing a wing with three different degrees of sweep, curving in a crescent from root to tip. Once again, the idea was not original; the Arado company had designed just such a wing shape in 1944.

The inboard, thickest part of the Handley Page wing was sharply swept at 35°; the thickness/chord ratio of 16% providing ample space for fuel, engines and main undercarriage, while at the tip the sweep was only 22°, with a thickness/chord ratio of 6%. This shape, without doubt the most advanced of any on British drawing boards in 1947, enjoyed a number of big advantages, not the least of which was that it had aeroisoclinic properties, eliminating a tendency to twist during high-G manoeuvres. By the end of 1947 the Handley Page design had assumed a more conventional appearance than the earlier tailless bomber, with a long fuselage and a tall, swept fin and rudder with a crescent-shaped, high-mounted tailplane. The aircraft, which was to have a crew of five, was to be powered by four 7,000lb st (31.15kN) Metrovick F9 or Rolls-Royce AJ65 engines; gross weight was to be 90,000lb (40,770kg) and, according to Handley Page estimates, it would be capable of carrying a 10,000lb (4,530kg) bomb load over a still-air range of 5,000nm (9,265km) at 520mph (832km/h) at 50,000ft (15,250m). The design was allocated the type number HP80.[12]

The official enthusiasm displayed over the 'futuristic' designs of both the Avro 698 and the HP80 almost strangled at birth the submission of another contender for a B35/46 contract — the design of Vickers-Armstrong (Aircraft) Ltd. The Vickers design team at Weybridge, under the direction of Rex Pierson, had begun jet bomber studies in 1944, at the same time going ahead with the development of a new piston-engined bomber, the Windsor. Early in 1945 everything looked promising for the Windsor: three prototypes had been built and flown, four more were in hand and 300 production aircraft were on order. Then came the war's end, cancellation of the order, and a halt to piston-engined bomber development, so Vickers accelerated its jet bomber programme under the direction of George R. Edwards, the new chief designer. The resulting design, the Vickers Type 660, was far more conventional than either the Avro or Handley Page aircraft, and although it offered vast performance and load-carrying increases over the Lincoln and B-29, it nevertheless fell short of the B35/46 requirement, so in July 1947 it was rejected in favour of the rival designs.

The new specification written round the Vickers Type 660, delineating its interim status, was B9/48, and in February 1949 two prototypes of the aircraft were ordered, one to be powered by Rolls-Royce Avon engines and the other by Sapphires, although it was later decided that both 660s should be fitted with Avons. Work on the aircraft had already started in April 1948, when the Ministry of Supply had issued an instruction to proceed (ITP), and now it continued around the clock, under conditions of the strictest secrecy, at Weybridge and Foxwarren, the Vickers dispersal plant where major components of most of the company's prototypes were built. In carrying out this task Vickers was fortunate in having some of the British aircraft industry's best research facilities, including a Mach 0.94 wind tunnel, installed in 1949.

The aircraft that took shape was highly streamlined and, for its size, remarkably elegant. The 108ft (32.94m) fuselage was of circular section, with a large navigation and bombing radar installation (the largest developed up to that time for a British aircraft) occupying the whole of the nose forward of the cockpit. A blister under the nose accommodated the visual bomb-aiming station. The pressurised crew compartment itself was built by Saunders-Roe, one of nine major subcontractors involved in the Type 660 programme, and accommodated five crew members: pilot and co-pilot, two navigators and an air electronics officer. The last three sat below and behind the pilots, facing aft, and had no ejection seats; in the event of an emergency they would have to unfasten their seat harnesses and various leads and open the main hatch, together with a metal windbreak that hinged out of the fuselage side ahead of the door. Without the windbreak, an exit from the hatch at high speed would have been virtually impossible. The two pilots would make their exit by first jettisoning the cockpit roof, which was blown off by a series of explosive bolts, and then using their Martin Baker Mk 3A seats.

Above:
The Vickers Valiant, first of the RAF's V-bombers, was a remarkably elegant aircraft. Photograph shows XD823, a production Valiant B Mk 1.
British Aerospace

In all fairness, it should be mentioned that in its original operational requirement, the Air Staff asked that the complete pressure cabin accommodating the crew should be jettisonable in an emergency and equipped with parachutes to form an escape capsule, but the contracting companies found the engineering problems associated with such a system to be insuperable. In 1948 Handley Page actually tested an escape system in model form, but the results were unsatisfactory and the idea was abandoned. Much later, in 1960, Martin Baker experimentally installed a rearward-facing ejection seat in Valiant WP199, a C of A (Controller of Aircraft) machine which had been modified for the purpose by Marshall's of Cambridge in 1959. There were delays in the programme because of pressure on Martin Baker for fighter aircraft ejection systems (they were developing one for the Mach 2 English Electric Lightning at that time) but trials

eventually took place in mid-1960 and on 3 June that year a slave seat was successfully fired from a static aircraft at Chalgrove airfield. There was, however, no further development of the project.

The Vickers Type 660's high-mounted wing had a mean sweep of 20°, the angle being increased towards the wing root — the thickest part — to improve lift-drag ratio. In this section the engines were buried. The structure of the wing, and indeed of the whole aircraft, was entirely conventional. In fact, the only major innovation lay in the electrical systems, with which the bomber was crammed. The main 112V dc system was supplied by four 22.5kW generators, one driven by each engine. Full voltage was obtained at all engine speeds from idling to take-off rpm. Most of the electrical equipment, and the main power distribution panels, were housed in an upper compartment (known to the crews as the 'organ loft') aft of the pressure cabin.

The prototype 660, WB210, was powered by four Rolls-Royce Avon RA3 turbojets of 6,500lb st (28.9kN). These were completely buried in the wing, with the tailpipes breaking the upper surface near the trailing edge. Originally, a single slot-type leading edge intake in each wing fed air to each pair of engines, but some initial difficulties with engine running led to vertical straighteners being added to the intakes before the aircraft made its first flight.

Early in 1951, the components of the prototype Vickers 660 were taken from Foxwarren to the new company airfield at Wisley, in Surrey, where final assembly took place. After a period of systems testing and pre-flight trials, WB210 made its first flight on 18 May 1951, with Vickers' chief test pilot J. 'Mutt' Summers as captain and G. R. 'Jock' Bryce as co-pilot. Four more flights were made from Wisley, but as this was only a grass airfield, the 660 was subsequently moved to Hurn while a runway was laid at the previous location.

In June 1951 the name Valiant was officially adopted for the Vickers design, and in 1952 it was decided that the Avro and Handley Page aircraft should have names beginning with V as well. The establishment of a 'V' class of medium bombers was proposed by the then Chief of the Air Staff, Marshal of the Royal Air Force Sir John Slessor, and in October 1952 the Air Council decided on the name Vulcan for Avro's B35/46, followed by Victor for the Handley Page design in December. This was a break with long tradition; hitherto, RAF bomber aircraft had been named after inland towns in the British Commonwealth (eg Canberra) or towns associated with British history (eg Lancaster). The Valiant flight test programme continued steadily with WB210 throughout the remainder of 1951. By this time a Royal Air Force officer, Sqn Ldr Brian Foster, had been attached to the Valiant test team, and on 12 January 1952 he was flying as co-pilot in the prototype, carrying out engine shutdown and relight trials over the Hampshire coast when fire broke out in an engine bay as the result of a wet start. No fire detection equipment had been installed in the bay, and by the time the blaze was detected the damage was so advanced that the wing was on the point of collapse. The pilot therefore gave the order to abandon the aircraft and the three rear crew members went out first, followed by the two pilots. All the crew survived with the exception of Sqn Ldr Foster, who was killed when his seat struck the fin while the aircraft was in a descending turn.

Fortunately for Vickers, the second prototype Valiant, WB215, was approaching completion, and this flew for the first time at Wisley on 11 April 1952. Allocated Type Number 667, WB215 differed from its predecessor in having enlarged air intakes to feed the 7,500lb st (33.4kN) Avon RA7 engines with which it was fitted. This aircraft sustained the test programme for more than a year and the Vickers team was joined by another RAF officer, Sqn Ldr Rupert G. W. Oakley.

On 8 February 1951 Vickers had received an Instruction to Proceed (ITP) for 25 production Valiant B Mk 1s, confirmed by a contract placed on 12 April. Five of these aircraft were to be powered by 9,000lb st (43.5kN) Avon RA14 engines, while the remaining 20 were to have 10,500lb st (50.1kN) Avon RA28s, with longer jet pipes. At about the same time, the company had also received a Ministry of Supply specification for the development of a prototype target-marking version of the Valiant, which was to be specially strengthened in order to fly low and fast and was to have increased fuel tankage. Bearing the Type Number 673 and the designation Valiant B Mk 2, this aircraft flew for the first time on 4 September 1953.

The strengthened airframe, coupled with Rolls-Royce Avon RA14 engines, gave the B Mk 2 version an enormous performance advantage over the earlier Valiant. It could, for example, attain a maximum speed at sea level of 552mph (835km/h), whereas the B Mk 1 was limited by airframe considerations to 414mph (662km/h). Performance of the production version, had it gone ahead, would have been even more impressive, for this was to have been powered by the Rolls-Royce RB80 by-pass engine, progenitor of the Conway turbofan. In the mid-1950s, however, the Air Staff decided that there was no longer a requirement for the role the Valiant B2 was to have fulfilled, and the sole example, WJ954, was eventually scrapped. Ironically, 10 years later the whole of the V-Force was compelled to adapt to the low-level role, and the airframes of the Valiants then in service were found to be incapable of withstanding the stresses imposed by prolonged low-altitude flight.

The first of the production Valiants, WP199, flew for the first time on 21 December 1953, well within the deadline imposed by the Ministry. Meanwhile, testing of the 'Blue Danube' was well advanced: aircraft and bomb were about to come together. It was not before time, for there was now an ominous threat from the east.

2 SOVIET STRATEGIC FORCES 1945-1955

In the evening of 30 July 1944, Soviet Yak-9 fighters were ordered to take off from the airfield of Spassk, close to The USSR's border with Japanese-occupied Manchuria, to intercept an unidentified aircraft which had just entered Soviet air space. To their surprise, the fighter pilots discovered that the aircraft was not Japanese, as they had expected, but an American B-29 Superfortress.

The aircraft, in fact, belonged to the 771st Squadron of the USAAF's 462nd Bombardment Wing, the first unit to equip with the new type. Operating out of Chengtu air base in southern China, it had been part of a force of 100 B-29s which, a couple of hours earlier, had attacked a Japanese steel mill at Anshan in Manchuria. The B-29 had been hit by an anti-aircraft shell over the target, and the pilot, realising that the aircraft would be unable to regain its base on three engines, had decided to follow the laid-down emergency procedure and head for Soviet territory.

The Russian fighters escorted the B-29 to a small airstrip near Tavrichanka, at the northern tip of Vladivostok Bay, and the pilot landed with considerable difficulty, bringing the aircraft to a stop only yards from where the edge of the field dropped away into the sea. A few hours later, the members of the crew were being interrogated by Soviet Air Force officers; it was to be several months before they finally left the USSR on their way home to the United States. They never saw their B-29 again.[13]

The unexpected arrival of the B-29 — which was followed by three more under similar circumstances during the remaining months of 1944 — was the answer to the Russians' prayers. As the war in Europe neared its end, the Chief Administration of the Soviet Air Force already had plans in hand for a substantial modernisation programme, and these included the formation of a modern strategic bomber force. In 1944, the only Soviet long-range bombers were the Petlyakov Pe-8 and Ilyushin Il-4, both of which were obsolete by comparison with Allied types; they formed the backbone of the Soviet Long-Range Aviation Force, the ADD, which earlier in 1944 had been redesignated the 18th Air Army and turned over to tactical bombing duties in support of the Soviet ground forces. With the wartime emphasis very much on the development of tactical bombers, assault aircraft and fighters, Soviet designers had had little time to study long-range bomber projects, and it was obvious that even if work on such projects began in 1944, there would still be a lengthy delay before a Soviet long-range bomber could be produced

in series. Then a ready-made answer, the B-29, literally dropped out of the Soviet sky.

By copying the B-29 in every detail, the Russians hoped to avoid all the technological problems associated with the indigenous development of such an aircraft. The designer chosen for the task was Andrei Tupolev, who had just begun work on the design of a long-range, high-altitude, four-engined bomber called the Tu-64 (which never got past the design stage and was abandoned in favour of the B-29 copy), while the job of copying the B-29's Wright R-3350 engines went to A. D. Shvetsov. The work was not easy; major snags cropped up frequently, particularly in connection with electrically operated equipment such as the B-29's gun turrets. Despite everything, however, construction of the prototype Soviet B-29 — designated Tu-4 — was begun in March 1945, and the first three prototypes were ready for flight testing at the beginning of 1947. The following year these three aircraft were publicly revealed at the big Soviet air display at Tushino, near Moscow. By this time series production of the Tu-4 was well under way and the first examples had been delivered to the Soviet strategic bomber force, the *Dal'naya Aviatsiya* (DA). The aircraft was externally similar to the B-29, except that the standard armament of 12 0.50in machine guns and one 20mm cannon was replaced by 10 NS-23 cannons.

Production of the Tu-4 (which was later allocated the NATO code-name 'Bull') was a very important milestone in the history of the Soviet aviation industry. Plants involved in the aircraft's manufacture had to learn more refined and precise methods; they also learned how to miniaturise certain items of equipment, and to impose stringent quality control in turning out material that had to be more finely machined than anything they had encountered so far.[14]

With the B-29/Tu-4, the Russians now had the means to deliver a nuclear weapon. By the time the Tu-4 entered production, Soviet nuclear research was well advanced, and the progress was made not entirely as a result of secret information passed on by Allied scientists who had been involved with the American atomic bomb project, although such leakages certainly played an important part. The Russians had begun active research programmes in nuclear physics in the 1930s, and in February 1939, when Soviet physicists learned of the discovery of nuclear fission from foreign scientific journals, they at once appreciated the potential military application. By April 1939, quite independently of any research elsewhere, they had established that the fission of each uranium nucleus emitted between two and four neutrons and that a chain reaction could be established using either Uranium 235 (U235) or natural uranium, and a moderator such as heavy water (deuterium oxide). German atomic research, it was later established, was proceeding along similar lines.

In June 1940 the Uranium Commission was established by the Soviet Academy of Sciences to carry out uranium research, the work involving exploration for uranium deposits, production of heavy water, construction of cyclotrons, the study of isotopic separation and measurements of the nuclear constants. The shortage of uranium deposits imposed a considerable restraint on early research, which ceased altogether following the German invasion of 22 June 1941. Early in 1942, however, the Soviet leadership began to receive intelligence reports of nuclear research programmes in Britain, the USA and Germany, and in 1943 Josef Stalin authorised the establishment of a small-scale project under the scientific direction of Igor Vasil'evich Kurchatov, who had been director of the nuclear laboratory at the Leningrad Physico-Technical Laboratory.

Kurchatov drew up a research plan with three main goals: to achieve a chain reaction in an experimental reactor using uranium; to develop methods of isotope separation; and to study the design of both U235 and plutonium bombs. By the end of 1943 he was directing a staff of 50 scientists, a figure that doubled in the following year. By the time of the Potsdam Conference, which opened as the first US atomic device was tested on 16 July 1945, the Soviet Union had a viable atomic bomb project under way. Eight days after the US test, on 24 July, President Truman mentioned to Stalin that the United States possessed a 'new weapon of unusual destructive force'. Stalin told Truman that he hoped the United States 'would make good use of it against the Japanese' and immediately instructed Kurchatov to accelerate his research programme.[15]

After the atomic attacks on Hiroshima and Nagasaki in August 1945, Stalin ordered Kurchatov's team to produce atomic weapons in the shortest possible time, and placed his secret police chief, Lavrenti Beria, in overall charge of the project. (German atomic scientists, it should be mentioned, had been compelled to obey the orders of SS Reichsführer Heinrich Himmler midway through World War 2, with disastrous consequences to the administration of their project.) Beria, however, proved a dynamic taskmaster, and by 1947 the institutional framework was in place to develop not only nuclear weapons but also rockets and jet propulsion.

In spring 1945 Kurchatov ordered work to begin on the design of an industrial reactor for producing plutonium. He also supervised the construction of an experimental graphite-moderated natural uranium pile (so avoiding the red herring of a heavy water moderator, which German scientists had been persistently following). Known as the 'Fursov Pile', or 'F-1', this was built in Kurchatov's Laboratory No 2, later to be called successively the Moscow Institute of Atomic Energy and later the I. V. Kurchatov Institute of Atomic Energy, and it was there, on 25 December 1946, that the first Soviet chain reaction took place.

The first Soviet atomic device (not yet a bomb) was detonated at the Semipalatinsk test site in Kazakhstan on 29 August 1949, and was code-named 'Joe 1' by the Americans. The test, which was a tower shot, used plutonium as the fissionable material and produced a yield of 10-20kT. A second device, 'Joe 2', was exploded on 24 September 1951 either on or slightly below the ground and produced a yield of at least 25kT, while 'Joe 3', detonated on 18 October 1951, was a composite design using both uranium and plutonium as fissionable materials.

Below:
The Tupolev Tu-80 was a redesigned version of the well-tried Tu-4 (B-29 copy). Two prototypes were built. *Author's Collection*

This shot produced a yield of 50kT and was probably the prototype of an operational bomb.[16]

Meanwhile, the Tupolev design team had been turning its attention to improving the basic Tu-4 design, the principal object being to increase the bomber's range. Retaining the basic structure of the Tu-4, Tupolev's engineers set about streamlining the fuselage, increasing its length by several feet and redesigning the nose section, replacing the Tu-4's rather bulbous cockpit with a more aerodynamically refined stepped-up configuration. The area of the tail fin was also increased and the fin made more angular in design. To reduce drag, the nacelles of the Ash-73TK engines (the Wright R-3350 copies) were redesigned. The outer wing sections were also redesigned and the span increased slightly, allowing for an increase in fuel tankage of 15%.

The redesigned aircraft, designated Tu-80, flew early in 1949. Two prototypes were built, and the operational version, while carrying a similar payload to that of the Tu-4, was to have had a defensive armament of 10 23mm cannon or 10 12.7mm machine guns in remotely controlled barbettes. By this time, however, the Soviet Air Force had begun to think in terms of an aircraft that would compare with the Convair B-36, which was beginning to enter service with SAC, and the Tu-80 was not ordered into production. Another Tu-4 derivative, the DVB-202, designed by Vladimir Myasishchev, suffered the same fate.[17]

In mid-1949, in response to the new specification, Tupolev embarked on the design of the biggest aircraft so far constructed in the Soviet Union, and the last Soviet bomber type to be powered by piston engines. At this time, several engine design bureaux in the USSR were working on powerful jet and turboprop engines that would power the next generation of Soviet combat aircraft, but it would be some time before these became operational, and in the meantime — with relations between East and West deteriorating rapidly, particularly as a result of the Soviet blockade of Berlin — the race to achieve parity with the United States assumed a high degree of urgency. This was especially true in the strategic bombing field; it was of little use if the Russians broke the American nuclear weapons monopoly by building up their own stockpile of atomic bombs, only to lack the means of delivering them to their targets. The B-36 had given SAC the capability to deliver nuclear bombs deep into the heart of the Soviet Union, but in 1949 the Soviets had no comparable bomber. The Tu-4 had the capacity to lift the USSR's early, cumbersome atomic weapons, but only over limited ranges; it could theoretically strike at targets in North America across the Arctic regions, but such a mission would be strictly one-way.

The new specification called for an intercontinental bomber capable of carrying an 11,500lb (5,209kg) bomb load over a combat radius of 4,375nm (8,106km) and then returning to

base without refuelling. Tupolev's answer was to produce a scaled-up version of the Tu-80 powered by new 4,000hp piston engines. In this way, Tupolev succeeded not only in retaining the proven aerodynamic and technical qualities of the Tu-80 and its predecessor, the Tu-4, but also saved time: only two years elapsed between the start of the intercontinental bomber programme and the first flight of a prototype. By way of comparison, it took the Americans five years to produce the B-36, although the latter was somewhat more revolutionary in concept.

The new bomber, designated Tu-85, began flight testing at the beginning of 1951, powered by four Dobronin VD-4K engines producing 4,300hp on take-off. The structure was light, employing a number of special alloys (although for some reason magnesium, which was used in the structure of the B-36, was not incorporated) and the long, slender, semi-monocoque fuselage was split into five compartments, three of which were pressurised and housed the 16-man crew. Defensive armament was the same as the Tu-4's, comprising four remotely-controlled turrets each with a pair of 23mm cannon. The roomy weapons bay could accommodate up to 44,000lb (19,932kg) of bombs. With an 11,000lb (4,983kg) bomb load, the Tu-85 had a range of 7,500nm (13,897km) at 295kt (546km/h) and 33,000ft (10,065m); normal range was 5,530nm (10,248km). Maximum speed over the target was 352kt (652km/h).

Several Tu-85 prototypes were built and test flown in 1951-52, but the aircraft was not ordered into production. Times were changing fast; in February 1951, before the Tu-85 began its flight test programme, the US Air Force had decided to order the Boeing B-52 Stratofortress, which was capable of attacking targets in the USSR from bases in the continental USA, and it was clear that the day of the piston-engined bomber was over. The Russians therefore decided to abandon further development of the Tu-85 in favour of turbojet-powered strategic bombers, although they fostered the impression that it was in service by showing the prototypes, escorted by jet fighters, at Aviation Day flypasts. The production of a strategic jet bomber was entrusted to Tupolev and also to the Myasishchev design bureau; the latter's efforts were to culminate in the four-engined Mya-4, which first appeared at Tushino in 1954 and received the NATO code-name of 'Bison'. Although never an outstanding success in the long-range strategic bombing role for which it was intended, the 'Bison' was nevertheless the Soviet Union's first operational four-engined jet bomber, and was roughly comparable with early versions of the B-52. Its main operational role in later years was maritime and electronic reconnaissance, and some were converted to the flight refuelling tanker role.

Tupolev's strategic jet bomber design was much more successful. Designated Tu-88, it flew for the first time in 1952 and entered service three years later as the Tu-16, receiving the NATO code-name 'Badger'. Owing much — in fuselage design at least — to the Tu-80, the Tu-16 was destined to become the most important bomber type on the inventories of the Soviet Air Force and Soviet Naval Air Arm for over a decade, with almost 2,000 aircraft produced overall.

Tupolev also adopted the Tu-85's basic fuselage structure in the design of a new turbojet-powered strategic bomber, the Tu-95. To bring the project to fruition as quickly as possible, the Tupolev team married swept flying surfaces to what was basically a Tu-85 fuselage. Development of the Tu-95 and Mya-4 proceeded in parallel, and it was intended that both types should be ready in time to take part in the Tushino flypast of May 1954. However, some delay was experienced with the Tu-95's engines, and in the event only the Mya-4 was test-flown in time. Flight testing of the Tu-95 began in the summer of 1954, and seven pre-series aircraft made an appearance at Tushino on 3 July 1955, the type being allocated the NATO code-name 'Bear'.

By this time the importance of the turboprop-powered bomber was growing, for the performance of the Mya-4 had fallen short of expectations and as a result production orders were cut back drastically. Even though the Tu-95's massive Kuznetsov NK-12 engines were still causing problems, it was realised that the Tupolev design would form the mainstay of the Dal'naya Aviatsiya's strategic air divisions for at least the next decade; an ironic turn of events, for in the beginning emphasis had been placed on the production of the Mya-4 in the mistaken belief that the turboprop-powered Tu-95 would be limited to a speed of 0.76M.

The USSR's new strategic bomber assets were divided in the main between three formations: the 30th Air Army (HQ Irkutsk), the 36th Air Army (HQ Moscow) and the 46th Air Army (HQ Smolensk). The 46th Air Army, forming the Western Theatre Strike Force, was numerically the most important, being eventually expanded to a strength of four bomber divisions, each consisting of 12 bomber regiments. The other Soviet air armies of the Cold War era, the 4th at Legnica in Poland and the 24th at Vinnitsa, were essentially tactical formations. The other tactical air army, the 16th, which was also the largest, was based in East Germany.

The bomber regiments were dispersed at 21 principal airfields around the perimeter of the USSR:

- Murmansk Northeast and Olenegorsk on the Murmansk peninsula.
- Vorkuta in the Soviet Arctic.
- Sol'tsy near Leningrad.
- Tartu and Chernyakhovsk on the Baltic.
- Lvov close to the Polish border.
- Bobruisk, Bykhov and Zhitomir in the Kiev region.
- Saki, Oktyabr'skoya and Adler on the Black Sea.
- Engels and Voronezh south of Moscow.

- Dolon, Belaya and Belogersk near the China/Mongolia border.
- Alekseyevka, Mys-Shmidta and Anadyr in the Far East.

Some of these bases were expanded wartime airfields, while others were newly built.

While the build-up of the strategic bomber force was progressing, so was the development of the USSR's nuclear weapons. On 12 August 1953, the Soviets exploded their first thermonuclear device; this was a fusion reaction with a boosted configuration involving the use of lithium deuteride, and produced a yield in the 200-300kT range. At about this time the Soviet Air Force received its first issue of atomic bombs, and in September 1954 the Soviets conducted their first large-scale exercise involving an atomic bomb detonation.[18] By 1955 small numbers of nuclear weapons were being produced for the army and navy as well as the air force, and in 1955 a series of tests took place involving the delivery of nuclear weapons by aircraft. These culminated in two significant shots, both occurring in November. The first, on the 6th, was apparently a thermonuclear bomb reduced in size to fit the bomb bays of The USSR's new generation of jet bombers; it produced a yield of 215kT. The second, which took place on the 22nd, was the first Soviet high-yield (1.6mT) weapon test and the detonation occurred at an elevation of several thousand feet. Subsequent analysis by the US Atomic Energy Commission showed that it was a two-stage bomb using both U235 and U233, as well as U238 and lithium deuteride. It was The USSR's 19th atomic test since 1949.[19]

Left and Below:
The Tupolev Tu-95 'Bear' was powered by four Kuznetsov turboprop engines. It made its first public appearance in May 1954.
Author's Collection

By the end of 1955, therefore, the Soviets had an effective nuclear strike force in place, and were about to deploy thermonuclear weapons. But the manned bomber was to have only a secondary place in the USSR's military strategy. At the end of 1945 the Russians had taken the decision to build their own versions of the German V-2 rocket, one produced by captured German scientists, the other by a Soviet group under the leadership of Sergei Korolev, a noted rocket scientist. Both missiles were tested in 1947 and the Soviet version proved to have a better performance than its German-designed counterpart; designated R-1, it formed the basis of all subsequent Soviet rocket development.

The relative success of the R-1 prompted a decision, taken in principle in 1947, to begin development of a weapon that could serve as an intercontinental ballistic missile (ICBM). According to one source, Stalin himself stated in 1947 that 'Such a rocket could change the face of war . . . The problem of the creation of transatlantic rockets is of extreme importance to us.'[20] The firm decision to throw massive funding into the development of an operational ICBM was taken in 1953, the year of Stalin's death. The decision pushed Soviet strategic planning along a road that was to be beset with technical difficulties and, for a critical period in the early 1960s, was to hand undisputed superiority in the dangerous world of nuclear confrontation to the Western Alliance.

3 BRITAIN'S DETERRENT
VALIANT DAYS

The onset of the Soviet blockade of Berlin in the summer of 1948 revealed how ill-prepared the Western Allies were to meet a major threat from the communist bloc, with their forces drastically run down since the end of World War 2. Once the threat had materialised, however, the Americans — and SAC in particular — were quick to react. The now-famous airlift was quickly established by the western powers, and steps were taken to prevent the Russians from interfering with it. This could only be achieved by dispatching modern combat aircraft to Europe with the utmost priority, and the spearhead of such reinforcement was the B-29, which had the capability to hit the Soviets hard. When the blockade began, one B-29 squadron of the 301st BG was on rotational training at Fürstenfeldbruck, Germany, and SAC immediately ordered the group's other two B-29 squadrons to move to Goose Bay, Labrador, to reinforce Germany if necessary. Two additional B-29 groups, the 28th and 307th, were placed on alert and ordered to be ready to deploy within 12 and three hours respectively. The rest of the SAC bomber force was placed on 24-hour alert.[21]

By early July, all three squadrons of the 301st Group were deployed at Fürstenfeldbruck, and on 16 July a joint announcement was made by the British Air Ministry and the US Air Force to the effect that two B-29 groups, totalling 60 aircraft, were flying from the USA to bases in England 'for a short period of temporary duty'; that this movement was 'part of the normal long-range flight training programme instituted over a year ago by the US SAC'; and that the groups would be based at RAF Marham in Norfolk and RAF Waddington in Lincolnshire under the operational control of Gen Curtis LeMay, Commanding General of the US Air Forces in Europe (USAFE). It was also announced that C-54 aircraft would be transporting maintenance men and supplies to the UK, that each B-29 would carry a regular and a spare crew, and that about 1,500 men would be involved in the deployment.[22] On 17 July 1948, 30 B-29s of the 28th BG, the first to be deployed, moved from Rapid City AFB, South Dakota, to their British base — not, as it turned out, either Marham or Waddington, but RAF Scampton, recently vacated by the Lancasters and Wellingtons of the Bomber Command Instrument Rating and Examining Flight. The next day, the 307th BG, comprising the 370th and 371st Bombardment Squadrons, brought its Superfortresses to Marham and Waddington. A third group, the 2nd, deployed to RAF Lakenheath in Suffolk later in the month. None of the B-29s deployed to Europe was nuclear-

Above:
This was the posture that had to be adopted by rear crew members in an emergency escape from the Valiant. The eyelid-type windshield is clearly visible. *Author's Collection*

Above Right:
The English Electric A1, the Canberra prototype, seen on rollout at Warton in May 1949. The Canberra provided valuable jet bomber experience for future V-Force pilots and navigators. *British Aerospace*

capable; in fact, only a relatively small number of SAC's B-29s were as yet equipped for the carriage and release of nuclear weapons, and these were retained on alert in the USA. In any case, no agreement existed at that time between the US and UK governments for the basing of nuclear weapons on British soil. The Russians, however, had to assume that the deployed B-29s were nuclear-capable, and the presence of even a small number of Superfortresses in Britain would, it was thought, have a considerable deterrent effect. Agreement had existed since 1946, though not on a formal basis, between the British Air Ministry and the USAF for the use of British air bases by conventionally-armed American bombers in the event of a war threat in Europe; its implementation was now little more

than a formality to which Clement Attlee's Labour government readily agreed.

Once installed, the three B-29 groups in England began a systematic training programme designed to familiarise the crews with the European environment — although some had seen service there during the war years — and also involving simulated bombing attacks on targets around the United Kingdom and elsewhere in western Europe. The original three groups remained in England for 90 days of temporary duty, setting the pattern for other SAC units that were to follow. At Scampton, the 28th BG's B-29s were replaced by those of the 301st BG from Germany; these departed in turn on 15 January 1949, whereupon Scampton reverted to RAF

use. At Marham, the 307th BG was replaced in November 1948 by the 97th BG, comprising the 340th and 371st Bombardment Squadrons. Only one other SAC B-29 unit, the 22nd BG (2nd, 19th and 408th Bombardment Squadrons) was to use Marham; subsequent TDY detachments operated the more advanced Boeing B-50.

The performance of the B-29 was greatly superior to that of the Avro Lincoln, the aircraft which at that time was the mainstay of RAF Bomber Command. Although the Lincoln could carry a substantial bomb load — 14,000lb (6,342kg) over a range of 1,953nm (3,618km) — it had a top speed of only 252kt (487km/h) and a service ceiling of 22,000ft (6,710m), all of which made it intensely vulnerable to air defences. With the first MiG-15s being deployed in Europe at the time of the Berlin Airlift, it is doubtful whether Bomber Command's Lincolns would have survived for long in hostile air space, had the crisis devolved into open warfare. In 1949, therefore, negotiations were conducted between the UK government and the USA for the supply of 87 B-29s under the Military Assistance Program. The first four aircraft, named Washingtons in RAF service, arrived at RAF Marham on 22 March 1950, and the whole force subsequently equipped eight medium bomber squadrons, with the exception of four aircraft used for electronic reconnaissance. In the following year Bomber Command received its first Canberra light jet bombers, which progressively replaced the Lincolns and Washingtons as more aircraft became available. In the meantime, SAC continued to hold the monopoly on the West's strategic deterrent, although that was soon to change.

In 1951, while development of the British atomic bomb proceeded at the various establishments of HER, the UK

Chiefs of Staff were considering the best location for the testing of the complete weapon. A request to use American test facilities with American collaboration in the test itself was turned down on the grounds that it might compromise US nuclear secrecy, and a possible site in northern Canada was rejected; it was the Admiralty who came up with a possible suitable location in the Monte Bello Islands, 50 miles off the northwest coast of Australia and about 700 miles (1,126km) north of Perth. The choice of this site was agreed in October 1951, not least because the Admiralty was keen to assess the effects of the detonation of a nuclear device on board a ship. The possibility of a surprise attack on a major port by this means had been considered, but its effects had not yet been studied by the Americans, so in a sense this would be a British 'first'.

The support personnel for the Monte Bello test — Operation 'Hurricane' — began leaving the UK in February 1952, led by Royal Engineers whose task it was to build roads and jetties and to erect accommodation and other buildings associated with the test. The 200 scientists, 50 technicians and 100 industrial workers needed for the trial left in April; their base was to be the former aircraft carrier HMS Campania, the principal support ship.

Early in June 1952 two nuclear capsules were loaded on to the frigate HMS Plym, the ship that was to be destroyed in the test, in the Thames estuary. When fitted with its fissile material, the warhead would weigh three tons, representing about two-thirds of the weight of the 'Blue Danube' bomb that would carry it in its operational form.[23] The task force, commanded by Rear-Admiral A. D. Torlesse, was well on its way by the time the plutonium for the fissile core arrived from Windscale for fabrication at Aldermaston. The task of ferrying it out to the test site was entrusted to Wg Cdr J. S. Rowlands, accompanied by Sqn Ldr P. E. Mitchell of the RAF team and W. J. Moyce, an explosives expert from Aldermaston. Rowlands later described the transportation procedure:

'The time factor made air transport essential and this was by Hastings and Sunderland aircraft. Each piece of radioactive material was transported in specially-designed containers which had to be crashproof, waterproof, fireproof and, very importantly, would float. Part of the brief in the Operation Order was that, if the aircraft had to ditch, Sqn Ldr Mitchell, Mr Moyce and I would cling on to these containers — which looked like very large dustbins — and ignore the sharks. Fortunately that contingency didn't arise. We took out two sets of components, one to act as reserve. I must have signed for these items because, a week or two after returning to the UK with the reserve set, Admiral Brooking of HER said I'd

better make a formal written statement that one set had been destroyed in a trial, otherwise the Treasury might pursue me for a million pounds or so.

'We moved the material to Lyneham by road and staged through Malta, Sharjah, Negombo and Singapore. Security was tight everywhere. Apart from the crew there were only three of us aboard the Hastings aircraft. In Singapore we landed at Seletar and, within minutes, we and the components had been transferred to a Sunderland aircraft riding at anchor in the Straits. We were airborne very quickly and flew uneventfully to land on the sea at Monte Bello.

'There we had some hectic work and rehearsals but were ready on D-Day. Some time beforehand the main task force retired a considerable distance away from Monte Bello leaving just a few of us aboard HMS *Plym* to await the go-ahead. In the still watches it was a somewhat eerie experience to be in the deserted lagoon, in an almost deserted ship shortly, we hoped, to be vaporized. The assembly went smoothly and we then abandoned HMS *Plym*. The only dangerous part of the operation was the long journey from Monte Bello to the task force in mountainous seas in a small boat . . .' [24]

At 09.30hrs local time on 3 October 1952 the device was exploded by cable from the island of Trimouille, 400yd (366m) away from the ship, sending up an expanding fireball and associated mushroom cloud to about 10,000ft (3,050m). Of HMS Plym, nothing remained. The detonation produced an estimated yield of around 25kT.

The success of the Monte Bello test meant that trials to prove 'Blue Danube's' ballistic case, radar fuse and contact fuses, firing circuits and in-flight loading of the nuclear element could now proceed, although it was realised that there would be a lengthy delay before the bomb could be matched with an operational Valiant B1, the aircraft that was to carry it. In fact, the bomb was delivered before the aircraft; the first atomic bombs for the RAF, or rather the components from which they would be assembled, were delivered to the Bomber Command Armament School at RAF Wittering in November 1953. The assembled 'Blue Danube' which was 12ft (3.66m) long, 5ft (1.5m) in diameter at the point where the nuclear capsule was fitted, and weighed 10,000lb (4,530kg) was a streamlined weapon with flip-out fins. It bore some resemblance to the wartime 12,000lb (5,436kg) 'Tallboy' bomb, which led to its being unofficially referred to as 'Smallboy' in the early days.

As no Valiant was yet available, ballistic trials with the 'Smallboy' were carried out by the very aircraft whose hopes of production the Valiant had destroyed, the Short SA4 Sperrin. On 11 April 1953 the second Sperrin, VX161, flew to RAF Woodbridge to begin ballistic tests, releasing bomb shapes of up to 10,000lb (4,530kg) at altitudes of up to 40,000ft (12,200m) and speeds of up to 0.78M. The first Sperrin (VX158) was meanwhile busy with operational trials of the new high-altitude radar navigational and bombing equipment that would eventually be incorporated in the

Vulcan and the Victor, markers being released through a small inset door in the bomb bay and a visual bombing station replacing the metal nose cone.

From April 1954, trials of the ballistics and internal equipment of the 'Blue Danube' MC Mk 1 special store came under the control of No 1321 Flight, formed at Wittering specifically for this purpose. The officer who was to command it (from June 1955) had already flown the 'special' Valiant, WP201, which was to be mated with an operational 'Blue Danube', at Wisley; he was Sqn Ldr D. Roberts, and on 15 June 1955 he and his crew (Flt Lts R. MacA. Furze, K. L. Lewis, T. E. Dunne and J. H. Sheriston) flew WP201 to Wittering to begin ballistic trials. On 6 July 1955, ballistic store B1 was successfully dropped from 12,000ft (3,660m).[25]

Meanwhile, in March 1954, the former wartime airfield of Gaydon, in Warwickshire, was reactivated after much rebuilding to become the first V-bomber base, and on 1 January 1955, after the Valiant had received its CA Release — ie clearance by the Controller (Aircraft) for operational service in the UK and overseas — No 138 Squadron was established there under Wg Cdr Rupert Oakley, who had been the RAF liaison officer at Wisley following the accidental

Above:
Flypast of the eight Valiants of No 138 Squadron, RAF Wittering. *MoD (RAF)*

Right:
Tail detail on No 214 Squadron Valiant, RAF Marham. *Author's Collection*

death of Sqn Ldr Foster. The squadron received its first Valiant B1 (WP206) on 8 February and its second (WP207) on the 19th, and two days later No 232 Operational Conversion Unit was established at Gaydon to convert crews who were beginning to arrive from the Bombing School at Lindholme, in Yorkshire.

Following a similar policy to that of America's SAC, all crews selected for service with the V-Force were to be veterans. Aircraft captains had to possess an 'above average' rating and had to have a minimum of 1,750 hours as first pilot; second pilots (called co-pilots from 1958) were required to have completed at least 700 hours as captain, and both must have completed a tour on Canberra light jet bombers. Navigators, too, had to have a Canberra tour behind them, as well as a course at the Bomber Command training school at Lindholme. Signallers — subsequently to be called air electronics officers (AEOs), which more adequately described their role — were required to have flown a tour with Bomber, Transport or Coastal Command. Originally, a V-Force tour lasted five years, compared with two and a half to three years elsewhere, and crews would often remain with the same squadron throughout that period. Later, with an increase in the demand for aircrew, the requirements for V-Force service were to become less stringent. The V-Force also introduced the American idea of the crew chief to the RAF. Usually a chief technician, he would be in charge of the ground crew assigned to an individual aircraft throughout its career, and flew in the aircraft on overseas trips.

In April 1955 No 138 Squadron received four more Valiants, and another (WP217) arrived in May, although this aircraft was earmarked for No 543 Squadron, which was shortly to be formed at Gaydon in the strategic reconnaissance role. In July No 138 began moving to its operational base at RAF Wittering, the first four Valiants flying in on the 6th. On the 29th, the squadron lost one of its Valiants, WP222, which crashed with the loss of all four crew soon after becoming airborne on a cross-country flight; the aircraft struck the ground in a steep descending turn, the cause later being determined as a runaway aileron trim tab actuator.[26]

The nucleus of the first operational Valiant squadron was now in place, and No 138 Squadron now embarked on an intense working-up period, being involved mainly in engine

Security at the V-Force bases was necessarily high. Here, an RAF policeman and his Alsatian stand guard beside a Valiant at Wittering. *MoD (RAF)*

Top:
Dispersal was a key element of
V-Force operational procedures.
The aircraft were usually
dispersed from their home bases
in clutches of four. Here, aircrew
are seen leaving their Valiants at
one of the 36 dispersal airfields
used by Bomber Command.
Author's Collection

This Picture:
A Valiant B1 on the approach to
Wittering, showing the aircraft's
large flap area.
Author's Collection

Right and Below:
HRH The Duke of Edinburgh
inspecting a Valiant of No 138
Squadron, 1955. *MoD (RAF)*

Left:
The Valiant's undercarriage was a robust affair, as this photograph shows. The officer on the right is Wg Cdr Rupert Oakley, OC No 138 Squadron. *MoD (RAF)*

Below:
Valiant crew of No 138 Squadron, 1955. Note the aircrew clothing of the time. *MoD (RAF)*

Top Left:
No 207 Squadron's first Valiant B1 arrives at RAF Marham, June 1956. *MoD (RAF)*

Below:
Valiant B1 WZ366, the first British aircraft to drop an atomic bomb (Maralinga, Australia, 21 October 1956). *MoD (RAF)*

proving trials during the remainder of 1955. On 3 September, the Valiant went overseas for the first time when WP206 and WP207 left Wittering for Habbaniya, Iraq, ground crew having been positioned along the route earlier. After a delay while WP206 had an engine changed at Sharjah, they flew on to Negombo, Ceylon, with a refuelling stop at Karachi; from there they went to Changi, Singapore, and then on to Australia, where they took part in displays at Sydney, Melbourne, Canberra and Hobart, Tasmania. The tour also took in New Zealand, where the Valiants demonstrated over Christchurch and Wellington before returning to Australia to give displays over Brisbane and Amberley. They began the return flight on 2 October, flying via Negombo and Karachi and reaching Abu Sueir, Egypt, on 4 October. From there, WP206 flew direct to Wittering, although WP207 had to make a brief refuelling stop at El Adem after developing a fault in the transfer fuel tank.

This operation, called 'Too Right', was a very useful proving flight for the Valiant, underlining the aircraft's ability to fly at high intensity in a variety of climates. Despite some unserviceability, the equipment on board the two aircraft had

worked well, particularly the STR18B2 radio equipment. The 'Green Satin' navigational radar system, although it had gone unserviceable in WP206 after 53 hours' flying, had 'behaved magnificently throughout the flight' in the other aircraft. All told, it had been a very encouraging exercise, and the flight had brought much prestige to the RAF. Most important of all, it had demonstrated that V-Force aircraft were able to deploy rapidly to distant parts taking their own support force with them — in this case, four Hastings transports of Nos 24 and 47 Squadrons.[27]

While No 138 Squadron worked up, No 1321 Flight's Valiant continued its ballistic trials work, which revealed the 'Blue Danube' to be very accurate. Its ballistics were so good that when it was released it had a tendency to keep pace with the Valiant, 'flying' beneath the tail area, so strakes were fitted to the underside of the fuselage forward of the bomb bay to disrupt the airflow and give the bomb a 'push' downwards. Between 15 June and 25 November 1955 No 1321 Flight dropped five Type B (for Ballistics) stores of 10,000lb (4,530kg) over the Orfordness range on behalf of the RAE as well as nine Type F stores designed to test the bomb's internal workings on behalf of the Atomic Weapons Research Establishment (AWRE). The drops took place at altitudes from 12,000ft to 47,000ft (3,660m to 14,335m).

In January 1956 No 1321 Flight, its trials work completed, was renamed C Flight of No 138 Squadron, which at the end of the month was up to full strength with eight Valiant B1s. Two more Valiant bases had now been established, at Marham in Norfolk and Honington in Suffolk, both within Bomber Command's No 3 Group area, and five more Valiant squadrons were to be formed in the course of the year. The first of these was No 214, which, having previously been equipped with Avro Lincolns, re-formed at Marham in March 1956 under the command of Wg Cdr L. H. Trent VC. It was joined, in May, by No 207 Squadron, which had previously been armed with Boeing Washingtons, also at Marham. Each unit was established for eight aircraft.[28]

On 1 May 1956, C Flight of No 138 Squadron became No 49 Squadron, which was to be the V-Force trials squadron. It was commanded initially by Sqn Ldr Roberts, who handed over to Wg Cdr K. G. Hubbard OBE, DFC on 4 September. The other two Valiant squadrons to form in 1956 were No 148 (Wg Cdr W. J. Burnett DSO, DFC, AFC) on 1 July, and No 7 (Wg Cdr A. H. C. Boxer DSO, DFC) on 1 November, the former at Marham and the latter at Honington.

By the end of the year, therefore, Bomber Command had six Medium Bomber Force Valiant squadrons and one (No 543) operating in the strategic reconnaissance role.

In October 1956 the Valiants of Nos 138, 148, 207 and 214 Squadrons, as we shall see in the following chapter, deployed to Malta in support of Operation 'Musketeer', the Anglo-French landings in the Suez Canal Zone. No 49 Squadron, meanwhile, had been preparing to deploy to Australia to participate in the first live trials of 'Blue Danube'. Four more British nuclear tests had been carried out since Operation

An early production Valiant B1. The aircraft had a very low ground clearance, as shown in this photograph. *MoD (RAF)*

'Hurricane'; the first two ('Totem' 1 and 2) were low-yield (10kT and 8kT) tower shots made at Emu Field, South Australia, in October 1953, and were unconnected with the 'Blue Danube' programme, but in May and June 1956 two more tower shots were made at Monte Bello, both designed to test warhead assemblies — designed by AWRE — in connection with the project to develop Britain's first thermonuclear bomb. The second of these tests, 'Mosaic' G2, produced a blast yield of 98kT and was centred on Alpha Island, Monte Bello. It was the largest (and dirtiest) test carried out on Australian territory.[29]

Four shots were programmed for the next series of tests, named 'Buffalo', and in August 1956 two of No 49 Squadron's Valiants, WZ366 (Sqn Ldr E. J. G. Flavell) and WZ367 (Flt Lt R. N. Bates) deployed to RAAF Edinburgh Field, from where they carried out numerous training sorties over the range facilities at Maralinga (where the test was to take place) and Woomera. These included four telemetred test drops, one with an inert (concrete-filled) round and three with HE warheads. After two tower shots ('Buffalo' R1 and R2), carried out on 27 September and 4 October 1956, the time came for 'Buffalo'

R3, the first British air drop of a nuclear device, on 21 October. The report describes the mission:

'At 14.00hrs . . . Valiant WZ366 took off from Maralinga airfield with the live nuclear weapon on board. The crew consisted of Sqn Ldr Flavell (captain), Gp Capt Menaul, Flt Lts Ledger and Stacey, Flg Off Spencer and Plt Off Ford. The aircraft climbed to 38,000ft (11,590m) in a wide arc, avoiding the range area until it reached the emergency holding area. The bombsight was levelled, contact was established with the air controller on the ground by VHF and HF, and the aircraft then descended to 30,000ft (9,150m) to begin the fly-over sequences, using precisely the same drills and procedures as in the concrete and HE drops. At 14.25 the first fly-over, Type A, was successfully completed, with all equipment, both in the aircraft and on the ground, working satisfactorily. Types B and C fly-overs were then completed in turn, and by 15.00hrs all was in readiness for the final Type D fly-over and the release of the nuclear weapon. The final D type fly-over was completed

according to plan with all equipment functioning perfectly, and the weapon was released at 15.27hrs. Immediately after release a steep turn to starboard on to a heading of 240° true was executed in order to position the aircraft correctly for the thermal measuring equipment to function. During this turn 1.9G was applied. The weapon exploded correctly and the aircraft, after observing the formation of the mushroom cloud, set course for base, where it landed at 15.35hrs. The operation had gone smoothly and exactly according to the plans drawn up during training. The bombing error was afterwards assessed at 110yd (100m) overshoot, and 40ft (12m) right. . .[30]

The 'Blue Danube' detonated at between 500 and 600ft (152 and 183m). The fissile material had been loaded into the nuclear capsule in flight and the weapon had a modified fusing system. Because of fears that the fusing system might fail, resulting in a 40kT ground burst and unwanted contamination, a low-yield (3kT) version was used, rather than a standard production bomb. Atomic cloud sampling

operations were flown by specially modified Canberras of No 76 Squadron, which had undertaken similar duties during 'Mosaic'. This squadron completed its task at Maralinga on 21 October 1956, sampling the mushroom cloud that resulted from 'Buffalo' R4, a 10kT tower shot.

By the time the 'Buffalo' tests were completed, development of Britain's first thermonuclear bomb was well advanced. The decision to go ahead with the programme had been taken on 16 June 1954 by Winston Churchill, the then Prime Minister, and a small Cabinet sub-committee. The Americans had successfully detonated an H-bomb on 31 October 1952, followed by the Russians ('Joe 4' on 12 August 1953) and Churchill had been impressed by the magnitude and implications of the new weapon, especially after reading the text of a speech made by Sterling Cole, 17 February 1954, Chairman of the Joint Committee on Atomic Energy of the US Congress. On 5 April 1954 Churchill addressed the House of Commons on the potential impact of the bomb.

After reaching the decision that the development of a British H-bomb was to proceed, Churchill was at pains to inform his allies; he told President Eisenhower about it on 26 June, and Canadian Premier Louis St Laurent three days later. Churchill's standpoint was clear, and it echoed that of his predecessor Clement Attlee: Britain could not expect to maintain her influence as a world power unless she possessed the most up-to-date nuclear weapons. There were also strong feelings at the time, both in the British government and in military circles, that Britain's possession of the H-bomb would exert a restraining influence on US policy. There was less concern at the time about Soviet aggression then there was over American adventurism.[31] The man in charge of development of the British thermonuclear bomb was W. R. J. Cook (later Sir William Cook), the Deputy Director of AWRE, who began active work on the project at Aldermaston on 1 September 1954, forming a Weapons Development Committee to plan the work and the necessary tests. Cook and his scientists cut a number of corners in developing a workable two-stage thermonuclear bomb in less than three years, and a lot of mystery still surrounds the precise way in which they achieved it. At least part of the solution may lie in the fact that there was now growing collusion in nuclear affairs between the British and Americans.

There was definite collusion early in 1954, when the Americans carried out a series of six tests — Operation 'Castle' — in the Pacific, the overall aim being to prove the feasibility of producing lightweight thermonuclear weapons. In the previous year, American observers had been permitted to attend the 'Totem' trials in Australia, a fact that was kept quiet for a long time, and, apparently as a reciprocal gesture, the RAF was allowed to fly cloud sampling missions during the 'Castle' tests.

The RAF unit involved was No 1323 Flight at RAF Wyton, which in February 1954 deployed two Canberra B2 aircraft (WH701 and WH738), each equipped with wingtip samplers

Above and Right:
Valiant B(K)1s of the Marham Wing. *MoD (RAF)*

and a small sampler attached to the underside of the fuselage, to the Pacific. All RAF insignia were deleted from the aircraft during the operation. The deployment was dogged by misfortune; on 23 February 1954 WH738 vanished without trace on a transit flight from Momote to Kwajalein, in the Marshall Islands, and on 11 March a replacement aircraft, WH679, lost its radio compass and had to make a forced landing on Ailinglapalap atoll, also in the Marshalls. The aircraft could not be salvaged, so its engines were removed and the airframe destroyed.[32]

These mishaps left only WH701 to carry out the sampling task, which it did on shots 'Bravo' (28 February), 'Romeo' (26 March) and 'Koon' (6 April). An engine failure just prior to take-off prevented its participation in 'Union' on April 25, but together with another replacement Canberra — WJ573, which arrived at Kwajalein on 27 May — it participated in test shots 'Yankee' (4 May) and 'Nectar' (13 May). Prior to each shot the RAF task force was given notice of the date and time of detonation, meteorological data and vectoring information that enabled the Canberras to track and intercept the clouds. The radio call sign 'Eager Beaver' was used on each operational sortie. Because the RAF operation was impaired by the loss of some of its aircraft, the Americans obligingly provided filter papers containing radiation samples collected by their own aircraft. All samples were flown back to the UK by Hastings aircraft on the day after each event.[33]

Scientific analysis of the samples almost certainly provided British scientists with valuable clues as to the nature of the American devices under test in the 'Castle' series, and may have contributed to the 'Mosaic' tests two years later. The first of these, 'Mosaic' G1 (16 May 1956) was designed to provide scientific data on thermonuclear reactions in light elements, and required small quantities of thermonuclear material — lithium deuteride — to be incorporated in the fission device to see if it could be ignited. This test produced a yield of 10kT, but the second test, 'Mosaic' G2 — as mentioned earlier — gave a yield of 98kT, and was probably a 'layer cake' assembly, with a layer of $U238$ surrounding a layer of lithium deuteride, which in turn surrounded the fissile core.

The 'Mosaic' results were to be crucial to the planning for the series of British thermonuclear tests, which were to begin just under a year later. In the meantime, 'Buffalo' had proved the 'Blue Danube' as a viable nuclear system, and the Valiant squadrons could now go ahead with defining operational procedures. A British deterrent was at last in place, but it was still the bombers of SAC which remained the western world's primary insurance against hostile attack.

4 BRITAIN'S DETERRENT
THE BLUE STREAK IRBM

The concept of a medium-range ballistic missile (MRBM) to supplement the manned bombers of the V-Force dated from August 1953, when the Air Staff launched a full evaluation of how to produce such a weapon. In April 1955, after lengthy preliminary studies, the de Havilland Propeller Co was asked to take on the responsibility of co-ordinating the design of the weapon system. The de Havilland Aircraft Co was to be responsible for the airframe, Rolls-Royce for the propulsion system, Sperry Gyroscope Co for inertial guidance and Marconi for ground radar and communications links. At the same time, Saunders-Roe was asked to build an experimental re-entry vehicle, designed by the Royal Aircraft Establishment. The concept was formalised on 8 August 1955, when the Air Staff issued Operational Requirement OR1139, calling for the development of a strategic missile with a megaton warhead (OR1142) and a range of 1,500-2,000nm (2,775-3,700km). The missile would be operated by Bomber Command and would be deployed to prepared sites in both the United Kingdom and the Middle East.

The missile that began to evolve, named Blue Streak, owed a great deal to the technology incorporated in America's first-generation ICBM, the Atlas. Development of the Atlas, the West's original ICBM, began in 1954, when the USAF realised that it had been mistaken in its earlier assessment of the ICBM's potential. The Convair Division of General Dynamics had already done a considerable amount of practical work with test vehicles — including one called MX-774, which tested such advanced features such as a gimbal-mounted engine, separable nose cone and a structure of very thin stainless steel. Convair was awarded the prime contract for the SM-65 Atlas, which came under the general heading of Weapon System 107A. Convair decided to adopt a thin-wall balloon tank, feeding five engines with Lox/RP-1 fuel; an LR89 sustainer motor rated at 57,000lb (253.5kN) thrust at sea level; two gimballed LR105 engines each rated at 150,000lb (667.5kN); and, for establishing the final trajectory, two small 1,000lb (4.5kN) LR101 vernier motors, all developed by Rocketdyne. All five engines drew propellants from the main tanks and all ignited simultaneously prior to lift-off. After about 140 seconds the boost assembly cut off and separated; the sustainer and verniers continued to burn for a further three minutes.

The first launch, of Atlas 4A with only the boosters fitted, took place from Cape Canaveral on 11 June 1957. The missile went out of control when one of the boosters failed soon after take-off, and it was destroyed by the Range Safety Officer. On 25 September Atlas 6A achieved partial success, and early in 1958 Atlas 12A was completely successful. On 2 August 1958 the second Atlas B missile flew 2,500 miles (4,022km), and the full design range of 5,500nm (10,175km) was achieved in November. The first launch of an operational Atlas D, by a crew of the 576th Strategic Missile Squadron (SMS) was made at Vandenberg AFB on 9 September 1959. The shot travelled about 4,300 miles (7,000km) at 16,000mph (25,744km/h).

At a very early stage in the British MRBM programme an agreement was reached between de Havilland and Convair, and also between Rolls-Royce and the Rocketdyne Division of North American Aviation, for an exchange of information. As development of the Blue Streak proceeded, those involved kept a close eye on the Atlas programme, and reaped the benefits of the flow of technological information. The pattern of the two development programmes followed each other closely, except that the Atlas was several years more advanced.

Each of the original Atlas strategic missile squadrons to be deployed, in 1958, had six missiles. The latter were sited entirely above ground in long shelters, which had sliding roofs to allow the missiles to be erected for fuelling and launch. The 549th SMS, which became operational in 1961, had semi-hardened installations recessed into the ground and was equipped with nine rounds. The RAF Air Staff was aware of American concern about the vulnerability of the Atlas's fixed, above-ground sites, and it was generally accepted that Blue Streak would be launched from underground sites.

By the end of 1957 the Blue Streak programme was progressing well, with the newly-formed Ballistic Missile Division of the Royal Aircraft Establishment (RAE) exercising technical supervision, and numerous Air Ministry meetings had been held to discuss matters concerning the weapon's operational deployment. It was estimated that the first test firing of a Blue Streak could probably take place from Woomera, Australia, early in 1962; the plan was for the operational missiles to be deployed in underground silos and raised to the surface immediately before firing. The operational missile sites would need to be at least six miles apart, and about 70 were required for the missile force to be fully effective.

While work proceeded on the Blue Streak missile itself, and planning for its deployment reached a fairly advanced stage, trials with its associated systems were also progressing. In

May 1957 the megaton warhead assembly (code-named 'Orange Herald') that was to be fitted to the missile was tested at Christmas Island during Britain's first thermonuclear weapons trials, dropped by a Vickers Valiant bomber of No 49 Squadron (Bomber Command's atomic test unit) and in September 1958 the re-entry test vehicle, 'Black Knight', was launched successfully from Woomera.

However, there was now growing concern over the rising costs of the Blue Streak programme. In the summer of 1957, as an economy measure, the Air Staff relaxed the accuracy requirement for Blue Streak, permitting the cancellation of two associated contracts: the Marconi radar guidance system and the English Electric backup inertial guidance system. In August 1957, a revised development programme was submitted to the Defence Research Policy Committee, limiting research and development costs to around £80 million, about

This Page:
The Victor K2 was a very capable tanker aircraft, and continued in the role right up to the Gulf War. *John Hardy*

half what would realistically be needed to complete the R&D programme. What it all added up to was that the Blue Streak programme was now seriously under-financed, with corners being cut everywhere as the purse strings were tightened.

With the development programme now proceeding at a dangerously slow pace because of the financial restraints imposed upon it, it was unlikely that the test-firing programme, which envisaged 23 shots by the end of 1963, would be completed. One area of concern was that more money needed to be spent on the engine test centre at Spadeadam, near Gilsland in Cumberland, where progress was painfully slow.

Already, by mid-1958, there was a school of thought that considered the development of Blue Streak as an operational weapons system should be abandoned. Various replacement options were proposed, including collaboration with the Americans in the development of a strategic rocket using a solid propellant, which would drastically reduce the necessary countdown time; another option was to purchase Thor IRBMs (which were then on the point of being deployed in the UK under joint Anglo-American control) outright from the USA and arming them with British warheads. The problem with Thor, apart from its vulnerability and slow reaction time, was that its useful life would not extend beyond 1964, and so there would still be a 'missile gap' before a new Anglo-American weapon could be deployed. As an interim measure, it would be necessary to proceed with the development of the advanced version of the British stand-off missile, Blue Steel Mk 2, in order to prolong the effective life of the V-Force until 1969 or thereabouts.

The British Minister of Defence, Duncan Sandys, a strong advocate of ballistic missiles, continued to argue in favour of Blue Streak; but he did not, as has sometimes been suggested, envisage the replacement of the manned bomber force by strategic missiles. Sandys wanted a diversified deterrent — manned aircraft and ballistic missiles — despite the fact that it would not be cheap if Blue Streak remained in the programme. Sandys took the operational credibility of the UK deterrent force very seriously, hence the expensive scheme for widespread bomber dispersal airfields, overseas as well as at home, and the adoption of the quick reaction procedures which Bomber Command perfected and demonstrated in training and exercises. He was determined that the deterrent should be seen to be effective as well as politically independent. However, Sandys did all he could to divert funds to the ailing Blue Streak programme, and one of the measures he took was to cancel further development of the Avro 730 supersonic bomber, envisaged as a replacement for the Vulcans and Victors in the late 1960s.

At a meeting of the Cabinet Defence Committee in September 1958, it was generally agreed that a land-based missile would be needed to maintain an independent British deterrent in succession to the V-Force's bombers, and that

work on Blue Streak should continue with a view to its deployment in 1965. There were, however, reservations. The Treasury estimated that the development and deployment of Blue Streak might cost as much as £600 million, and the cost might rise appreciably higher if underground launching sites were constructed. The other options — which by now included Polaris, the submarine-launched ballistic missile in whose development the UK was participating with the US Navy — still merited further investigation.

In April 1959 the Air Council endorsed the principle of underground deployment for Blue Streak, but Treasury approval for this was not forthcoming. There were other factors to be considered, too, such as the purely physical one of where the missiles were to be deployed in the UK. A wide dispersal policy was obviously necessary, but the UK enjoyed none of the USA's broad geographical advantage. A geological survey had already shown that much of the eastern half of England was geologically unsuitable, as the underground silos needed to be sited in rock masses 300-500ft (90-150m) thick (which is why the French, at a later date, sited their IRBMs in the Plateau d'Albion in Haute Provence), and there would probably be widespread public opposition to the construction of missile silos elsewhere.

The final battle lines around Blue Streak were drawn in July 1959, when the British Nuclear Deterrent Study Group began a thorough assessment of the deterrent's future. The group's conclusions, in a report at the end of 1959, was that Blue Streak would not be vulnerable once it had been launched, but that it would be vulnerable to pre-emptive attack whether deployed above or below the surface. It would therefore be effective only as a first-strike weapon, say in response to a Soviet conventional attack, and in that case it would not strictly be necessary to deploy it underground.

The report further recommended that if the UK deemed it acceptable to be totally dependent on the United States for a strategic missile force from about 1965, then an approach should be made to the US government with a view to arming the V-bombers with the Douglas WS138A Skybolt air-launched IRBM, or to acquiring the Polaris SLBM, together with a number of strategic missile submarines.

Although some, with Duncan Sandys (now Minister of Aviation) at the forefront, continued to argue for the retention of Blue Streak, it was effectively doomed as an operational missile. From March 1960, when Prime Minister Harold Macmillan conferred with US President Dwight D. Eisenhower at Camp David, the UK government set its feet firmly on the road that was to lead to Skybolt and ultimately, when Skybolt was cancelled, to Polaris.

Blue Streak was cancelled in April 1960, having cost the British taxpayer £89 million in research and development. The rocket itself survived, as a first-stage booster in the European Space Programme, until it was eventually replaced by the French Ariane.

5 VALIANT COMBAT:
SUEZ, 1956

Although it had nothing to do with the Valiant's nuclear attack role, the deployment of the aircraft to Malta as part of the Anglo-French air build-up for offensive operations against Egypt following the latter's seizure of the Suez Canal Company's assets in the summer of 1956 merits coverage, for it was the first and only time that the Valiant saw action, and its operations over Egypt revealed some weaknesses in the conventional bombing role.

Above and Below:
Valiants at RAF Luqa, Malta, during Operation 'Musketeer'. *MoD (RAF)*

The Valiant squadrons deployed to Malta in connection with Operation 'Musketeer', as the Anglo-French punitive expedition was known, were No 138 (Wg Cdr R. G. W. Oakley DSO, DFC, DFM) from RAF Wittering, and Nos 148 (Wg Cdr W. J. Burnett DSO, DFC, AFC), 207 (Wg Cdr D. D. Haig DSO, DFC), and 214 (Wg Cdr L. H. Trent VC, DFC), all from the

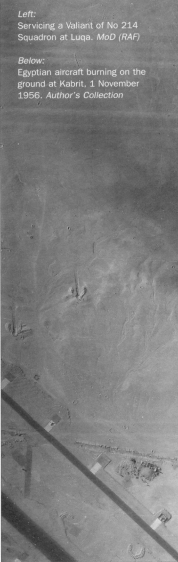

Left:
Servicing a Valiant of No 214
Squadron at Luqa. *MoD (RAF)*

Below:
Egyptian aircraft burning on the
ground at Kabrit, 1 November
1956. *Author's Collection*

Marham Wing. By the time the deployments were completed, Malta was host to 92 bombers, of which 25 — the Valiants — were at Luqa, the remainder being Canberra B6s.

In accordance with Phase One of the 'Musketeer' plan, the object of which was the elimination of the Egyptian Air Force before it could interfere with the Allied convoys sailing towards their objectives along the Egyptian coast or with the air drops, the bombing of the Egyptian airfields was scheduled to begin at 16.15hrs GMT on 31 October. Before that, while daylight lasted, 11 reconnaissance sorties were flown over the target areas, four by Canberras and seven by French RF-84Fs. The overall PR coverage was excellent, and was to remain so throughout the campaign, although not all the results reached the right people. As Sqn Ldr Paul Mallorie of No 139 Squadron (Canberras) remembered:

'Intelligence was very sparse . . . when we came to study our targets what we had to look at were old pages torn out of pilots' handbooks from the time the British were there. We did not see, in the whole of the operation, a single current photograph of the airfields and defences that we were going against, although we did see photographs of our raid results afterwards.'

Some photographs of relevance were also provided by the US Central Intelligence Agency, operating the high-altitude

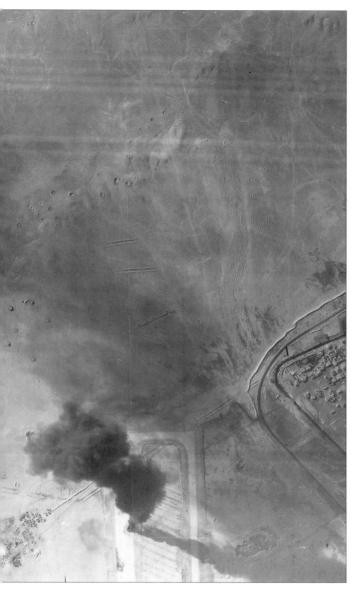

Lockheed U-2 reconnaissance aircraft on surveillance missions over the Middle East, but the importance of these has been exaggerated; it was the Canberras and RF-84Fs that brought back the photographic intelligence of real value. The important point about the exchange of information between the Americans and Anglo-French command was that it continued throughout the operation, despite the severe differences at senior political level.

When Air Marshal Denis Barnett, the Air Task Force Commander, launched his Canberras and Valiants against the airfields on 31 October, the target marker Canberras from Cyprus actually took-off after the main force had left, as the B6s were going in at low level and therefore did not have to

climb to altitude and form up. The plan called for the Valiants from Malta, which were equipped with the combined Navigation and Bombing System (NBS) — only recently fitted and as yet not very reliable — to drop proximity markers that would guide the marker force to its targets.

Things went wrong from the beginning. As No 139 Squadron's Canberras were about to leave their dispersals, the crew of the aircraft piloted by Flt Lt John Slater, whose target was Cairo West, were startled to hear a banging on the fuselage door. It transpired that, earlier in the day, Anthony Eden, the British Prime Minister, had been approached by the US Ambassador in London, who was concerned for the safety of US citizens being evacuated from Cairo to Alexandria by a road that passed very close to Cairo West. In fact, the road had been rebuilt and rerouted and was now a good 10 miles clear of the airfield, but nobody realised this; the maps that had been consulted were out of date. The result, in Whitehall, was something close to panic, and a most urgent signal was sent to General Sir Charles Keightley, the Supreme Allied Commander, instructing him to cancel the Cairo West attack. Unfortunately, it was not sent to the commander of the Air Task Force, who was controlling the operation; by the time it filtered through, the Malta force was already on its way and the Cyprus Canberras were just getting airborne. Lewis Hodges, a group captain and station commander at Marham who had gone out to Malta with the Valiant Wing, recalls that:

'. . . we never received any instructions at all through the normal command chain from Cyprus, but I received a personal signal direct from the Chief of the Air Staff, Sir Dermot Boyle, saying that on no account was Cairo West airfield to be bombed that night. The first wave of Valiants was on its way to Cairo; this created enormous problems, because of course there were four or five subsequent waves due to take-off immediately afterwards. I initiated an immediate recall of the first wave on WT, but in addition the flight path of the aircraft was very near to El Adem and we were in communication with El Adem to give a verbal instruction by RT in plain language to recall these aircraft to Luqa. This was successful and the aircraft were recalled, but we had a situation where eight Valiants were returning to Luqa with full bomb loads and further waves were taking-off to go to Cairo. We had to have the bombs jettisoned and you can imagine the problems of landing these aircraft, with others taking-off, on a single runway. It was a very difficult operation and the air traffic control at Luqa, which was RAF but working with the Malta Civil Aviation Authority, did a marvellous job.'

The target was hurriedly switched to Almaza, for which Flt Lt Slater and his crew now headed. The Canberras of the main force destined for Cairo West were also switched to Almaza, and by the time the signal reached them they were only 10 minutes away from the target area, which gave their navigators a great deal of work to do in very little time. The

Left and Below:
Valiant crews debriefing at Luqa after a sortie over Egypt.
Author's Collection

Right and Far Right:
Cairo International Airport after a bombing attack, 7 November 1956.
Author's Collection

outcome was that, although Almaza was successfully marked, and although there was good air-to-air communication between the marker aircraft and the main force, the latter erroneously bombed Cairo International Airport, which was adjacent to Almaza. The latter airfield was attacked in a second raid some three hours later, and considerable damage was caused.

Canberras and Valiants also attacked Kabrit, Abu Sueir and Inchas on this first night of operations. Although keeping a constant lookout for MiG-15s and Meteor night-fighters proved a great distraction to the crews (and contributed to the confusion that resulted in the bombing of Cairo International), the anticipated reaction from the enemy defences failed to materialise. In fact, Cairo and every town in the Nile Delta was ablaze with light; only after the first bombs fell did the Egyptians impose a blackout. The sighting of a solitary Meteor NF13 was reported by the crew of a No 148 Squadron Valiant, but the Egyptian aircraft was well below the bomber's 40,000ft (12,200m) altitude and made no attempt to attack.

At first light on 1 November, the land-based and carrier-borne strike squadrons took over the task of eliminating the Egyptian Air Force. Targets to the west of the 32° line of longitude were attacked by the Royal Navy's fighter-bombers, while those to the east were hit by the RAF Venom ground attack aircraft from Cyprus, French F-84F Thunderstreaks being assigned to the top cover role.

Between dawn and dusk on this first full day of operations the Royal Navy flew 205 strike sorties and the RAF 106; the French F-84Fs added 75 to this total. At the end of the day,

Allied intelligence became aware that very few of Nasser's Soviet-supplied Il-28 jet bombers had been destroyed or damaged; air reconnaissance revealed that most of them had been evacuated to Luxor, situated about 270 miles (435km) up the Nile valley south of Cairo. This was beyond the range of the ground attack aircraft, but it could still be reached by the Valiants and Canberras, and as the Il-28s still posed a substantial threat to the Cyprus base, Luxor was placed on the target list for the night of 1/2 November.

Both bomber wings were fully employed in the airfield attacks that night. Twenty-four Canberras and Valiants attacked Cairo West, 18 Canberras and Valiants went to Fayid, 16 Canberras and Valiants to Kasfareet and 24 Canberras to Luxor. In all, they dropped 429 1,000lb (453kg) bombs on the four airfields.

Crews returning from Luxor reported that the airfield had been badly hit, but post-strike reconnaissance by a No 13 Squadron Canberra at 12.40hrs GMT on 2 November told a different tale. No bombs had fallen on the airfield, and the Il-28s were all intact.

Phase Two of the air attack plan, which was to have been implemented on 2 November, had envisaged attacks on selected key point targets, some in urban areas, associated with a psychological warfare campaign designed to reduce the Egyptian will to resist. World opinion, however, coupled with a growing reluctance by the British government to risk unnecessary civilian casualties, resulted in a last-minute change, and General Keightley issued instructions that only military targets were to be attacked during this phase.

By nightfall on 2 November the Egyptian Air Force, with the exception of the Il-28s at Luxor (which would later be destroyed by French F-84Fs operating from Cyprus) had been virtually eliminated, and from now on the brunt of the air operations would be borne by the fighter-bombers. The Valiants continued to operate at a reduced rate. At 16.45hrs GMT on 4 November, seven Valiants and nine Canberras from Malta and four Canberras from Cyprus attacked the radar and coastal gun emplacements on El Agami island in a softening-up operation prior to the seaborne landings. Anti-aircraft fire was heavy — probably the heaviest encountered in the whole campaign — but no aircraft were damaged. An hour later, six Valiants and 12 Canberras from Malta, backed up by four marker Canberras from Cyprus, pounded Huckstep Barracks, this time with little opposition.

On 6 November, with British and French paratroops consolidating their objectives in the Port Said area and the seaborne landings about to begin, bombing attacks by the Valiants and Canberras ceased in accordance with instructions from London, and the following day three Valiant squadrons, Nos 138, 214 and 207, left Malta to return to their UK bases, while in the next 24 hours three Canberra squadrons, Nos 10, 15 and 44, departed Nicosia for the United Kingdom. As a precaution against renewed hostilities, however, 20 Valiants and 24 Canberras continued to be held at varying states of readiness in the United Kingdom, and all shore-based aircraft remaining in the Mediterranean stayed at their 'Musketeer' locations, releasing the Royal Navy's carrier-borne aircraft. Following these redeployments, air operations in the Eastern Mediterranean were limited to photographic and tactical reconnaissance and transport support, the latter assuming great significance with the continuing presence of British and French troops in and around Port Said and the occupation of Gamil.

For the RAF, there were lessons to be learned from the Suez operation. Not the least of them was that the early airfield attacks by the main force aircraft of RAF Bomber Command were conspicuous only by their failure, although others might term them a 'partial success'. The fact remains that in 18 raids on 13 targets, the Valiants and Canberras dropped 1,962 bombs, and of these — according to subsequent calculations by the Bomber Command Operational Research Staff — 70% fell in the target area but only 50% fell within 650yd (595m) of the aiming point. This was partly attributable to the fact that the Valiant crews were not yet fully worked up with their navigation and bombing systems, and the Canberra crews had to depend on visual bomb aiming, as their normal GH ground

navigational aids were not available in the Middle East. Another problem with the Valiant was a tendency for part of the HE bomb load to hang up, and at high speed the bombs tended to stay with the aircraft immediately after release, suspended in the airflow. The problem was eventually cured by the fitting of baffles. One of the most important lessons of 'Musketeer', however, was that it emphasised the value of retaining an independent nuclear deterrent. At the climax of the operation, when the Soviets were making thinly-veiled threats of atomic retaliation against London and Paris, Britain's nuclear weapons were still in the testing stage, apart from a small stockpile of the first British atomic bomb (the MC Mk 1 'Blue Danube'), and France had yet to test her first nuclear device. Even a nuclear force only fractionally as large as that of the Soviet Union still represented a powerful insurance against nuclear blackmail. As a result of 'Musketeer', the French accelerated their atomic weapons programme, which culminated in their first nuclear test in 1960, and before the end of 1956 they had issued a requirement for a nuclear delivery system, which resulted in the Dassault Mirage IV strategic bomber.

While the French decided to go their own way in the aftermath of Suez, the US and UK began to make concerted efforts to improve all aspects of their relationship. Three important meetings during 1957 laid the groundwork for the full resumption of co-operation in the nuclear weapons field. The first meeting, between British Defence Minister Duncan Sandys and Charles Wilson, US Secretary of Defense, was held between 28 January and 1 February in Washington. Several important subjects were discussed, including the adaptation of British bombers to carry US nuclear weapons, the storage of US nuclear bombs on British territory and the co-ordination of bombing targets between the SAC and Bomber Command.

The second meeting, between President Eisenhower and Harold Macmillan (who had replaced the ailing Anthony Eden as Prime Minister in January 1957) took place on 21-24 February in Bermuda. From this meeting came the public announcement that American Thor IRBMs would be deployed to the UK. There were also two other matters covered in a secret annex, one regarding prior consultation on testing initiatives and the other concerning a common policy towards French nuclear ambitions. Another meeting between the two leaders, in Washington on 23-25 October, led to a 'Declaration of Common Purpose' which was to be a turning point in the sharing of information on nuclear matters. If 'Musketeer' had caused a rift in Anglo-US political relations, little healing was necessary on the military front.[34]

6 ENTER THE VULCAN AND VICTOR

On 30 August 1952, the delta-wing bomber designed by A. V. Roe and Co to specification B35/46, the Avro 698, made its first flight from Woodford in Cheshire, with Chief Test Pilot Roly Falk at the controls. The maiden flight was not without incident, the aircraft losing the fairing panels behind both main undercarriage legs as it flew round the circuit, but there was no danger to the aircraft and Falk made a safe landing.

After appearing at the Farnborough Air Show in September, the Type 698 — VX770 — was grounded for modifications to the instrument panel and other changes that included the installation of a seat for the second pilot. It was flying again by the end of October — by which time the name Vulcan had been bestowed upon it — and continued the test-flying programme until May 1953, when it was grounded once more to be fitted with 7,500lb st (33.8kN) Armstrong Siddeley Sapphire 6 engines.

The original intention had been to fit the prototype with Bristol Olympus engines, but these were not ready in time, and so VX770 had flown with 6,500lb st (31.4kN) Rolls-Royce

Below:
The two Vulcan prototypes, accompanied by all four Avro 707 research aircraft, at the 1953 Farnborough Air Show. *British Aerospace*

Above:
The Avro 698 Vulcan prototype, VX770. The aircraft exploded in mid-air and crashed at Syerston during an air show in 1958; it was then being used for engine trials.
British Aerospace

Left:
XA891 was the first production Vulcan B1 and was used for Olympus 200 engine development. It crashed in Yorkshire on 24 July 1959, the crew escaping unhurt.
British Aerospace

Top Right:
Avro Chief Test Pilot Roly Falk amazed Farnborough crowds by upward-rolling the Vulcan at the 1955 SBAC show.
British Aerospace

Right:
This photograph shows the Vulcan's entry/exit hatch, in very close proximity to the nosewheel undercarriage. The officer is Group Captain Finch, OC RAF Waddington, and the Vulcan is on a goodwill visit to RAAF Richmond, Australia.
MoD (RAF)

Avon RA3s. The Olympus was finally ready for service in 1953, and was installed in the second prototype Vulcan, VX777, which flew for the first time on 3 September 1953.

The installation of the new engines in the second prototype meant that a lot of extra development work had to be carried out. The aircraft's pressurisation and radar systems also had to be fully tested at this stage, because it was intended to use VX777 for high-altitude handling trials and trials of the navigation/bombing radar, VX777 being the first Vulcan to have a visual bombing 'blister' under the nose. All these plans received a severe setback when, on 27 July 1954, VX777 was badly damaged in a heavy landing at Farnborough, leaving VX770 to carry on the development programme until its sister aircraft could be repaired. The accident caused serious delays to the engine development programme, but some of the planned high-altitude trials were carried out by VX770, the aircraft being pushed to its maximum speed. Some quite severe buffeting was experienced at speeds of 0.80M to 0.85M, and it was calculated that this could lead to fatigue in the outer wings. However, trials already carried out with wind tunnel models indicated that the buffet threshold could be pushed back substantially by redesigning the outer wing, and the Phase 2 Wing, as it was known, was devised so that the outer leading edge, from 48.5% semi-span to the tip, was extended forwards by the addition of a newer and thinner downward-drooped leading edge.

The result was a wing that swept sharply at 52° to 48.5% semi-span, 10° less sharply to 78% and then at 52° once more to a somewhat broader tip, producing a pronounced 'kinked' effect. The wing was approved for all production aircraft, although the approval came too late for its introduction on the first few production machines, which were then flying or about to be rolled out.

The first production Vulcan B1, XA889, flew for the first time on 4 February 1955, powered by four new twin-spool Olympus 101 engines rated at 11,000lb st (46kN). The second production aircraft, XA890, appeared at Farnborough that year and was upward-rolled before the crowds by Roly Falk, clearly demonstrating the big aircraft's manoeuvrability. Flight testing, meanwhile, continued with the two prototypes, VX777 having rejoined the programme in February.

As was the custom, a team of RAF personnel had worked closely with the Avro team during the Vulcan test programme. It was led by Sqn Ldr Charles C. Calder, who first flew the delta with Roly Falk on 18 February 1953. By the end of 1955, a considerable nucleus of RAF crews had gained experience on the Vulcan, and more followed when the first production aircraft, XA889, was delivered to Boscombe Down for service acceptance trials in March 1956. By that time, other Vulcans were being delivered to the various Ministry of Supply establishments to play their parts in the acceptance programme.

Royal Air Force crews, coming fresh to the Vulcan from the twin-jet Canberra light bomber, found a number of surprises in store. The first was the immense wing area and the general height of the aircraft from the ground — at least 6ft (1.83m). Moving rearwards from the nose, past the bomb-aimer's blister, one came to the entrance door, with the stalk of the twin-wheel nosewheel assembly just behind it — an arrangement that caused some misgivings at first to the rear crew members, who felt that they might have trouble abandoning the aircraft if the wheels were down.

Moving further back under the 3,550sq ft (330sq m) of wing, the next eye-catcher was the main undercarriage, built by Dowty, each leg having eight wheels on a levered-suspension bogie carried on a big magnesium alloy casting. The wheel wells also contained the refuelling and defuelling panels. The fuselage fuel bay was located immediately aft of the pressure cabin, and behind this was the 29ft (8.8m) weapons bay, which, as an alternative to special stores, could accommodate 21 1,000lb (453kg) bombs in clutches of seven. The weapons bay, because of its height above the ground, had to be loaded from trolleys by hydraulic jacks working directly on the bomb beams.

The crew of the Vulcan entered the pressure cabin via the underside door, which swung down to an angle of 45° and had a ladder inside, one section of which slid down to hang vertically from the door's lower edge. Inside the cabin, just above and aft of the door, the two navigators and the AEO sat in bucket seats in line abreast on a raised platform, facing rearwards towards their equipment consoles. The two pilots climbed another ladder to the flightdeck; getting into their ejection seats required some contortion, as they had to squeeze past a central console that carried the throttles and various other items of equipment. Apart from that, the cockpit was well laid out, with full dual controls; the control column was of the type usually associated with fighter aircraft, having pistol grips instead of the more normal 'spectacles', and the

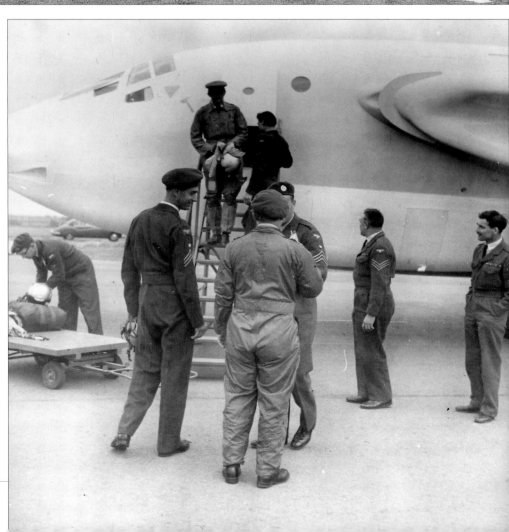

Top Left:
Overseas 'Lone Ranger' flights by single aircraft were an important aspect of V-Force training. Here, Vulcan B1 XH502 of No 617 Squadron is seen visiting Taiwan on a Far Eastern tour. The aircraft in the foreground are Chinese Nationalist F-86F Sabres. *Author's Collection*

Above:
The Handley Page HP88 research aircraft was used to test the crescent wing design used in the Victor bomber. *Author's Collection*

Right:
Entry to and exit from the Victor was by means of a side hatch. The Victor's cockpit layout was the best of the three V-bombers. *Author's Collection*

This Page and Top Right:
Vulcans on the assembly line at
Avro's Chadderton factory.
British Aerospace

throttles were centrally placed between the pilots. The throttle quadrant also housed the four fuel gauges, airbrake switches and the parking brake lever. The engine instrument panel was directly above it, with the pilots' blind flying panel on either side. There were neither controls nor instruments on the cockpit roof.

The captain's console on the port side of the cockpit incorporated the radio, engine starting, bomb door and power-flying control panels, while on the opposite side the second pilot was responsible for pressurisation, de-icing and air conditioning. The only real criticism of the cockpit was its restricted view; because the canopy was completely opaque there was no vision overhead or to the rear, the blankness being broken only by two small circular side panels. Through these, by leaning as far forward as possible and turning his head, the pilot could just see the wingtips. The view forward was also restricted by the position of the cockpit coaming, the angle at which the big delta 'sat' on the ground and the height of the cockpit, which could make marshalling a tricky procedure, especially in rain. It also created a problem when checking the correct function of the power controls, because the pilot was unable to see them. The usual procedure, after engine start, was for the crew chief — standing outside the aircraft, with his intercom plugged in — to confirm their operation, and as an added check the pilot had a visual indicator on the engine control panel. This was rather like an artificial horizon, with the addition of a tail fin and moveable indicators on the wings to represent the flying control surfaces.

Taxying was relatively uncomplicated. Once the aircraft was moving, it would continue to roll to the take-off point at idling rpm and the nosewheel was fully steerable, its operation controlled by a spring-loaded push-button on each control column. The take-off checks were also simple, and once they were completed the Vulcan was lined up on the runway and the engines opened up to full power while the pilots maintained pressure on the toe brakes. The nosewheel was used to steer the bomber until the rudder began to bite at around 60kt (111km/h), the stick being held forward to keep the nosewheel on the ground until unstick speed was reached. A slight backward pressure was then enough to lift the aircraft off the ground.

Apart from its high degree of manoeuvrability and its rate of climb, which was quite exceptional for an aircraft of its size in the mid-1950s, another remarkable quality about the Vulcan was its rate of descent. In a maximum-rate descent the bomber could lose 20,000ft (6,100m) in only 90sec, recovery to level flight being established in only about 1,500ft (457m).

Their experiences with the Vulcan left the RAF Handling Squadron crews at Boscombe Down with the impression that the introduction of the bomber into squadron service would be an uncomplicated process, and that it would be well capable of carrying out the tasks assigned to it.[35]

The Vulcan obtained its service release on 31 May 1956, being cleared, among other things, for speeds up to 0.98 indicated Mach number and flying at an all-up weight of 167,000lb (75,650kg) with full internal fuel and a 10,000lb (4,530kg) bomb load. On that same day, No 230 Operational Conversion Unit (Wg Cdr F. L. Dodd DSO, DFC, AFC), which had previously trained Lincoln crews at RAF Upwood, re-formed at RAF Waddington, Lincolnshire, to train Vulcan crews; two Vulcans, XA895 and XA897, were allocated to the

Left:
The Victor's high-set tailplane greatly enhanced the aircraft's aerodynamic characteristics on landing, which was usually effortless.
Author's Collection

Below:
A Victor in formation with RAF Hawker Hunter jet fighters.
Author's Collection

Right:
Flanking a Hawker Hart biplane, two representative aircraft of the V-Force, a Victor and Valiant, are pictured at Honington on the occasion of the presentation of the Queen's Standard to Nos 55 and 57 Squadrons on 20 July 1962. The Valiant is, in fact, a No 90 Squadron aircraft. *John Hardy*

Operational Conversion Unit (OCU) some weeks later, but it was decided to keep them at the Aircraft and Armament Experimental Establishment (A&AEE) Boscombe Down while Operational Reliability Trials were carried out. In the event, XA897 never reached the OCU. On 1 October 1956, while on approach to land at London Airport in low cloud and rain at the end of a very successful goodwill flight to New Zealand, it struck the ground short of the runway and crashed, killing four of the six people on board. The two who escaped were the aircraft captain, Sqn Ldr Donald Howard, and his VIP co-pilot, Air Marshal Sir Harry Broadhurst, the AOC-in-C Bomber Command.[36]

It was not until January 1957 that No 230 OCU received its two Vulcans: XA895 and XA898, the latter replacing the unfortunate XA897. Five more Vulcans were added to the OCU's strength by the end of May 1957. The first course qualified on 20 May and immediately formed A Flight of No 83 Squadron (Wg Cdr D. A. Frank DSO, DFC) which, following two years' disbandment since operating the Avro Lincoln, now became the first RAF squadron to arm with the Vulcan. A second squadron, No 101 (Wg Cdr A. C. L. Mackie DFC) — a former Binbrook-based Canberra B6 unit, which had disbanded nine months earlier — re-formed at Finningley in Yorkshire on 15 October 1957, and on 1 May 1958 a third squadron, No 617 (Wg Cdr D. Bower OBE, AFC) also rearmed with the Vulcan B1 at its original home, RAF Scampton, near Lincoln. In the months to come, these three squadrons, armed with the 'Blue Danube', gradually assumed the role of spearhead of the British nuclear deterrent.

By this time, RAF Bomber Command had begun to receive the third of its trio of V-bombers, the Handley Page Victor B1.

The prototype HP80 Victor, WB771, was flown from Boscombe Down on 24 December 1952 by Handley Page's Chief Test Pilot, Sqn Ldr H. G. Hazelden, with E. N. K. Bennett as his flight observer. The maiden flight was effortless, and it was during the landing that the Victor displayed one of its finest handling characteristics; if set up properly on final approach it would practically land itself. When most aircraft entered the ground cushion in the round-out stage just prior to touchdown, the ground effect tended to destroy the downwash from the tailplane, causing a nose-down moment and making it necessary for the pilot to hold off with backward pressure on the control column; the Victor's high-set tailplane eliminated this effect almost entirely. Also, the aircraft's crescent wing configuration reduced downwash at the root and upwash at the tips, a characteristic of normal swept wings, and this produced a nose-up pitch that contributed to a correct landing attitude.

The HP80's structure was every bit as remarkable as its aerodynamics, and incorporated many features which were radical departures from any previous techniques. The wing was of multi-spar construction with load-carrying skins forming multiple torsion boxes; the inner part of each wing was of three-spar construction, with a four-spar structure outboard of the landing gear. The all-metal ailerons operated through Hobson electrically-actuated hydraulically-powered control units; there were hydraulically-operated Fowler flaps on the inboard trailing edges, with two-piece hydraulically-actuated leading edge flaps on each outer wing (these were later replaced by 'drooped' leading edges). The wing itself was of sandwich construction, with a corrugated core of aluminium alloy sheet for the skin and components such as

Above:
Victors of No 15 Squadron on detachment to RAF Butterworth, Malaysia. One aircraft is leading a flypast of RAAF Canberras and Sabres, with RAF Javelin all-weather fighters bringing up the rear. *Via Jim Bowman*

ribs and spar webs, resulting in considerable strength combined with weight saving. The wing box ran ahead of the engines, which were completely buried in the thick inboard section of the wings; there was adequate room for the installation of larger and more powerful units, and less risk of damage to the wing box if an engine caught fire or a turbine disintegrated. Much use was made of spot welding in attaching the outer skin to the core of the wing, a very bold move on the part of Handley Page at that time.

The fuselage assembly comprised three major components: front, combined centre and rear, and tail cone. The front fuselage housed the pressure cabin, containing most of the operational equipment and the crew of five; as in the Valiant and the Vulcan, the two pilots had ejection seats and the three rear members had swivel seats, facilitating their exit through a door in the port side of the cabin. The cockpit layout of the Victor, however, was different from that of the other two V-bombers in that the Victor crew were not at markedly different levels; the two pilots, in fact, were seated very slightly lower than the three rear crew members. Climbing into their ejection seats was far easier for the pilots than was

the case with the Valiant or Vulcan, as they did not have to negotiate a central console; in the Victor, this could be pushed forwards and up towards the main panel, locking down into position when the pilots were seated.

The main fuselage section was taken up almost entirely by the enormous weapons bay, which was almost twice as large as that of the Vulcan — an advantage made possible by the crescent wing structure, which permitted the box-section fuselage joint to be set well forward. The bomb bay was completely unobstructed, its roof supported by four fore-and-aft girders which were attached to box-section frames providing the main supports for the bombs. In the conventional bombing role, the aircraft could carry 35 1,000lb (453kg) bombs. The bomb doors retracted into the fuselage in operation.

The fuselage centre section was joined to the rear section by a bulkhead which was specially stressed to accept tail loads. The rear section housed an equipment bay, tail radar, large hydraulically-operated air brakes and the base structure of the T-tail unit. Like the wings, this was a cantilever all-metal structure with corrugated sandwich skin panels.

Finally, the landing gear, designed by Electro-Hydraulics, consisted of two main units, each with eight-wheeled bogies on an oleo-pneumatic shock absorber and retracting forwards; and the nosewheel, a twin-wheel assembly with hydraulic steering, retracting backwards.[37]

By the time the prototype HP80 made its first flight, Handley Page had received an order (dated 14 August 1952) for 25 production aircraft. Some of the delays of the previous year had now been offset by a relatively trouble-free flight test programme, which was proceeding on schedule. The only real snag occurred during the aircraft's fourth flight, when the main undercarriage tyres burst following a landing with brakes on. On 25 February 1953 WB771 was flown to the Handley Page aerodrome at Radlett, which was now to be its base following extensions to the main runway. By the end of June it had cleared handling and systems and had also carried out many other trials, some involving crew escape.

Much of the test programme late in 1953 was occupied with trials of braking parachutes, a maximum of four being deployed; trials were also carried out with drogue parachutes fitted to the jettisonable cockpit roof, the idea being that these would lift the roof clear of the tail unit when it was 'blown'. February 1954 saw the aircraft engaged in high-speed manoeuvring trials at high altitude; the flight crews reported that the aircraft handled well in steep turns at speeds of up to 0.895M.

Trials so far had revealed the need for some structural modifications, including some to the tailplane. So that the flight test programme might proceed with the minimum delay, the tailplane from the second prototype, which was still under construction, was fitted to WB771 in place of the original one, and the programme was soon resumed.

On 14 July 1954, WB771 was carrying out a test programme that involved a series of high-speed, low-level runs along the runway at Cranfield to carry out Air speed indicator (ASI) position error checks. On one run the horizontal assembly started to flutter, then the tailplane and elevators broke away and the Victor dived into the ground, impacting on the runway intersection. The aircraft was totally destroyed and the crew killed instantly. The cause was later attributed to fatigue failure of the three bolts which joined the tailplane to the fin.[38]

The second Victor, WB775, flew on 11 September 1954. After carrying out handling trials at Radlett and Boscombe Down, it was given a thorough overhaul and some modifications were made to its fin, including the fitting of a thicker skin. It was airborne again on 1 February 1955, and two days later it began a series of trials involving the opening

and closing of the weapons bay doors in flight. After a small number of sorties the aircraft was grounded while the flash bomb bay doors were sealed, as there was no longer a requirement for this installation. Modifications were also carried out to the bulkhead at the rear of the weapons bay, as tests with models had shown that the original configuration would have created a dangerous water trap, dragging down the Victor's nose in the event of a ditching.

On 14 March 1955 WB775 went to Boscombe Down for preliminary trials with the A&AEE, and in June some 'Blue Danube' air drops were carried out over the Orfordness range. The second prototype Victor subsequently led a fairly routine life, testing a variety of systems until it was eventually dismantled at Radlett in 1959.

The first production Victor B1, XA917, flew for the first time on 1 February 1956, fitted with 11,000lb st (49kN) Armstrong Siddeley Sapphire 202 engines (the prototypes had used Sapphire 100s) and was retained by Handley Page for trials. On 1 June 1957 it became the largest aircraft at that time to exceed the speed of sound, reaching 1.1M in a shallow dive at 40,000ft (12,200m). This was quite accidental, and it was a tribute to the Victor's aerodynamic qualities that the crew had no warning other than the Machmeter indication that Mach One had been exceeded: the aircraft remained completely stable throughout and the control functions were perfectly normal.

The Victor B1 received its CA Release for Service use on 29 July 1957, although there were many restrictions; 10 pages of modifications needed to be carried out before the aircraft would be acceptable for delivery to the RAF, and it was not until 9 October that Victor B1 XA930 arrived at Boscombe Down for Operational Reliability Trials. On 21 November, No 232 OCU at Gaydon — the former Valiant OCU, which was now to handle the Victor — began No 1 Victor Course, its first aircraft, XA931, arriving on the 8th. The first Victor OCU course qualified in April 1958 and the majority of its graduates went to the first Victor squadron, No 10 (Wg Cdr C. B. Owen DSO, DFC, AFC) which received its first aircraft at RAF Cottesmore on 9 April.[39]

The second Victor B1 squadron, No 15 (Wg Cdr D. A. Green DSO, OBE, DFC) formed at Cottesmore on 1 September 1958, and the third, No 57 (Wg Cdr K. C. Giddings OBE, DFC, AFC) at RAF Honington on 1 January 1959. As No 57 Squadron had yet to receive its aircraft, the strength of the V-Force at this time stood at seven Valiant, three Vulcan and two Victor squadrons, with 82 aircraft and 104 crews. As yet, it was still very much an interim force; real viability would come with the eventual introduction of the Mk 2 versions of the Vulcan and Victor, armed with weapons of infinitely greater destructive power than the 'Blue Danube'.

7 THE 'GRAPPLE' TRIALS

While the V-Force worked its way towards achieving an initial operational capability, the design of a British thermonuclear bomb was progressing, and in 1956 plans were laid for a series of megaton-weapon tests in the Pacific Ocean, to take place in the following year. The operation, which was to involve participation by all three Services, was originally called 'Green Bamboo'; this was later changed to 'Gazette', and finally to 'Grapple'. The main base for the tests was to be Christmas Island, in the southwest Pacific; the actual test site was to be Malden Island, 350 miles (563km) to the south. Christmas Island, so named because Captain Cook had landed there on Christmas Eve 1777, was a classic coral island, and was made habitable for the trials by the efforts of the Royal Engineers. All units involved were grouped under Task Force 308 (Air Vice-Marshal W. E. Oulton).

Once again, all air drops during the series were to be carried out by the Valiants of No 49 Squadron, and in March 1957 four aircraft were deployed to Christmas Island. Many preparations had to be carried out before the first live drop, such as the installation and checking of telemetry equipment,

Below and Opposite:
Two views of XD818, the aircraft that dropped the first British H-bomb, resplendent in white paintwork at the 1959 Battle of Britain display, RAF St Athan, and in camouflage as 'gate guardian' at RAF Marham. It is now on display at the RAF Museum, Hendon. *Author's Collection*

and the Valiant crews underwent two months of intensive training. In fact, the Squadron had been training for the event since the previous September, but had been unable to complete its training programme in the UK because of bad weather.[40]

Among the aircraft supporting the trials were the Canberra B6s of No 76 Squadron and the PR7s of No 100 Squadron, which came under the control of No 160 Wing, as the Air Task Group was designated. Because of the expected magnitude of the megaton explosions, and the high-altitude levels of the resulting mushroom clouds, it was anticipated that the Canberras would have problems in reaching the required operational altitude of 56,000ft (17,080m) during their radiation sampling missions, and so plans were made to fit a double Napier Scorpion rocket motor in two of No 76 Squadron's aircraft. The liquid-fuelled Scorpion, selected originally to give extra boost at altitude to the English Electric Lightning interceptor (but never used, because the Lightning could easily reach 70,000ft (21,350m) or more on the power of its Avon RA24s alone) was test-flown in May 1956 in Canberra B2 WK163, and in its Double Scorpion form it helped power this aircraft to a new world altitude record of 70,310ft (21,445m) on 28 August 1957.

The two Canberras of No 76 Squadron fitted with the Double Scorpion installation were WT206 and WT207. A third

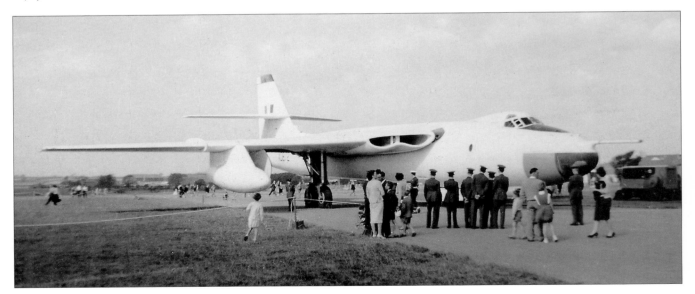

aircraft, WT208, was experimentally fitted with a de Havilland Spectre rocket motor, but was not assigned to TF308. No 76 Squadron's contribution to Operation 'Grapple' was six Canberras, while four PR7s were provided by No 100 Squadron. In addition, two Canberra PR7s of No 58 Squadron were earmarked to fly the radioactive samples back to the UK for analysis; the canisters were carried in a girder-like modification (known as the 'Forth Bridge') in the aircraft's bomb bay.

On the morning of 15 May 1957, Valiant XD818, captained by Wg Cdr K. G. Hubbard OBE, DFC, took-off from Christmas Island to carry out the first live drop of the 'Grapple' series. The other crew members were Fg Off R. L. Beeson (second pilot), and Flt Lts A. Washbrook DFC (navigator), E. J. Hood (observer) and E. Laraway (signaller). Take-off was at 09.00 (local time). The official report on the drop reads:

'The bombing run was made at 45,000ft true, and as Green Satin drift was fluctuating badly, the set was put to Memory on an average drift. The bombing run was steady on a course of 203°T and the weapon was released at 1036 "W" time. Immediately after release the aircraft was rolled into the escape manoeuvre which averaged a turn of 60° bank, excess G 1.8 to 1.9, airspeed 0.76M, rolling out on a heading of 073°T. The time taken for the turn was 38sec, and at the time of air burst of the weapon, the slant range between aircraft and burst was 8.65 n/ms.

'Neither crew nor aircraft felt any effect of flash, and the air blast reached the aircraft 2.5 min after release; the effect of the blast was to produce a period of 5 sec during which turbulence alike to slight clear air turbulence was experienced.

'Six minutes after weapon release, all shutters in the aircraft were removed, and after one orbit to see the mushroom cloud effect, the aircraft returned to base and made a normal landing.'[41]

The purpose of this detonation was to test a high-yield fission bomb using a 'Short Granite' warhead based on the 'layer cake' principle. The various components of this particular device were flown to Christmas Island aboard two 'courier' Valiants, each aircraft carrying a separate part of the bomb, and the device was assembled in two parts in special AWRE laboratories on the island. The whole assembly was called 'Green Granite'. Prior to the 15 May drop there were three other trials: on 3 May Valiant XD822 dropped a 10,000lb HE store to test the equipment associated with the 'Orange Herald' assembly being developed for the Blue Streak medium-range ballistic missile; on 5 May XD824 carried out a similar trial associated with 'Green Bamboo', the assembly under development for a free-falling megaton weapon and air-launched missile; and on 11 May XD818 dropped a complete 'Green Granite', but with a high explosive warhead. 'Blue Danube' ballistic cases were used in each assembly.[42]

The 'Short Granite' detonation of 15 May, which occurred at an altitude of about 8,000ft (2,440m), produced a yield of 100-150kT. It was later publicised as a 'megaton' device, which it was not. It was a so-called 'fall-back' fission device, a lightweight fission bomb producing a considerably higher yield than the first-generation atomic bombs.

When the Canberra B6s of No 76 Squadron returned to Christmas Island after their radiation-sampling cloud penetrations (which they made at altitudes of up to 54,000ft (16,470m), with oxygen turned fully up and navigators constantly monitoring the radiation dosage) they taxied to the decontamination centre on the south side of the airfield. Handling crews, dressed in full protective clothing, extracted the filters from the sampling equipment, labelled them and packed them into heavy lead canisters. The aircraft themselves were washed down with high pressure hoses which stripped off their special layer of barrier paint and also washed right through the engine intakes and turbines.

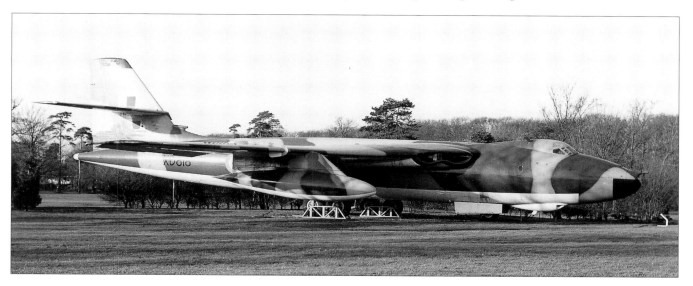

Canberra PR7 WT503 of No 58 Squadron (Flt Lts R. E. Taylor and P. Bruce-Smith) was positioned alongside the decontamination centre and after the canisters were loaded into its 'Forth Bridge' girder, it took-off for Hickam AFB, Honolulu, on the first leg of its flight back to the United Kingdom. It was followed by WT504 of No 100 Squadron in case it went unserviceable at Hickam, but all went well and it took-off on the five-and-a-half hour leg to Travis AFB, California. Here the aircraft was taken over by another crew, who flew it to Goose Bay via Namao; on this sector it was followed by PR7 WH790, also of No 58 Squadron. Tragically, this aircraft crashed nine miles from Goose Bay while overshooting in a blizzard, killing both crew. WT503 made three approaches before it got down safely. After refuelling it proceeded on the final stage of its journey to the UK.

On 18 May Valiant XD824 dropped a 10,000lb (4,530kg) HE 'Orange Herald' assembly, and on 23 May XD822 dropped two inert 'Blue Danubes'. Two days later the same aircraft dropped an HE 'Green Bamboo' assembly, followed by an HE 'Orange Herald' on 28 May. This was a prelude to the first live 'Orange Herald' drop, also by XD822, on 31 May. The pilot was Sqn Ldr D. Roberts, veteran of the early 'Blue Danube' trials, who experienced a few unpleasant moments when the aircraft went into a high-speed stall during the turn away after bomb release because of the failure of a crucial instrument, the accelerometer. Roberts quickly regained control, averting a situation that might easily have led to structural failure of the aircraft. The device, which comprised a fissile core contained within hollow hemispherical explosive sections, covered by two copper hemispheres, detonated as planned and produced a yield of 150-200kT.

The third drop in this initial series of 'Blue Danube' tests took place on 19 June 1957, when Valiant XD823, piloted by Sqn Ldr A. G. Steele, released a device fitted with a 'Purple Granite' warhead. This produced a yield of 75-100kT.

At the end of this phase, it was clear that all had not gone well with the 'Grapple' tests,[43] and that further experimentation was required to provide a greater understanding of the triggering mechanisms that were needed to produce high-yield thermonuclear explosions. To this end, a series of tests called 'Antler' was set up at the Maralinga range in Australia, the first taking place on 14 September 1957. This used a small, lightweight device called 'Pixie', with a plutonium core and an experimental small-diameter implosion system. The tower shot produced a yield of about one kiloton. Two more tests were conducted at Maralinga: the first, on 25 September, was 'Indigo Hammer', a 6kT plutonium device that could be used either as a fission primary for a thermonuclear weapon or as a warhead for a surface-to-air missile (in this case the Bristol Bloodhound, which was on the point of being deployed for the air defence of V-bomber bases), and 'Antler' Round 3, a 25kT fission primary test that involved a device suspended under a balloon. This device, which contained a plutonium core in a highly enriched uranium shell, was exploded on 9 October 1957.

Testing at the Pacific Range resumed on 8 November 1957, when Valiant XD825 flown by Sqn Ldr B. T. Millett dropped a fission device in 'Grapple X'. The explosion produced a high yield — possibly as high as 300kT, according to some estimates — and was probably the first really successful test to have taken place at Christmas Island.

What is thought in some quarters to have been the first true British two-stage thermonuclear test 'Grapple Y' took place on 28 April 1958, when Valiant XD824 (Sqn Ldr R. N. Bates) dropped a 'Granite'-type bomb that detonated with an estimated yield of 2mT. The next shot ('Granite Z'/'Pennant 2', on 22 August 1958) was another test of a fission primary, the device — which produced a yield of between 26 and 42kT — being suspended from four barrage balloons; then, on 2 September, came 'Grapple Z'/'Flagpole 1', when Valiant XD822 (Sqn Ldr G. M. Bailey) dropped a 2.5mT bomb by radar, the error from 45,000ft (13,725m) being only 95yd (87m). On 11 September a bomb of similar yield was dropped by Valiant XD827 (Flt Lt S. O'Connor), confirming that Britain was now a full member of the thermonuclear club. It was Britain's last atmospheric thermonuclear test, and on 23 September another nuclear (26-42kT) balloon shot completed the 'Grapple' trials.[44]

The first step on the road that led to the 'Grapple' trials was taken on 6 April 1955, when the Chiefs of Staff decided that the development of a weapon with a yield of about one megaton should receive first priority. On 28 July 1955 the Ministry of Supply accepted Air Staff Requirement OR1136, calling for the development of a thermonuclear bomb, with an in-service date of 1959 envisaged. By spring 1956 drawings and a mock-up of the bomb — codenamed 'Yellow Sun' — had been completed at RAE Farnborough, and another bomb, a kiloton-range weapon called 'Red Beard', was also under development as a potential replacement for 'Blue Danube'.

In October 1956, the Director-General of Armament and Weapons at the MoS suggested that an interim megaton warhead might be brought into service before 'Yellow Sun', and that if the 'Grapple' trials were successful the production of a form of megaton warhead could begin in August 1957. The warhead, which would be fitted into a 'Blue Danube' bomb case, could be either 'Green Granite', 'Green Bamboo' or 'Orange Herald'.

The suggestion was adopted, and in March 1958 the first such interim weapon, known as 'Violet Club', was assembled at the Bomber Command Armament School at Wittering. It was identical to the 'Blue Danube' except for its warhead, which was a pure fission type called 'Green Grass'. It was not really a megaton weapon at all, the warhead having a yield of around 300kT, but the British conveniently defined 'megaton range' as a few hundred kilotons to several megatons. It was cheating a little, but it did not matter; the RAF would soon have its true megaton weapon, and in the meantime 'Violet Club' — a very sensitive weapon that was very difficult to handle — increased the British deterrent capability. Very few were delivered, and they were withdrawn from service in 1959, with the issue of the first 'Yellow Suns'.[45]

8 SHAPING THE FORCE:
ALERTS AND EXERCISES

For RAF Bomber Command, the late 1950s, following the introduction of the Valiant, were marked by a period of experiment and development, with the intermarriage of old and new operational techniques. Taking into account the Valiant's performance, which was a vast improvement over that of any previous RAF bomber, conventional bombing techniques remained basically similar to those in force since the latter part of World War 2, as the Suez operation had demonstrated; after 1956, however, the advent of nuclear weapons made greater demands on crews and aircraft, and accordingly a new set of operational procedures had to be devised.

The rearming of No 3 Group, commanded by AVM K. B. B. Cross CB, CBE, DSO, DFC from 3 February 1956 to 4 May 1959, with the Valiant was accomplished in a remarkably short time, although some of the equipment which was regarded as essential — the navigational bombing system, for example — did not arrive until later. With the aircraft in place, No 3 Group's task was to turn the force into an operational reality, first of all in its nuclear role and secondly in its conventional role.

A typical Valiant training sortie during this period would involve a 4-4.5hr cross-country flight, with simulated radar bombing attacks against targets around the UK. The busiest crew members before such a sortie would be the navigators, the navigator (radar) assembling information on the assigned radar targets and the navigator (plotter) noting all relevant route information, including weather details. The co-pilot was responsible for all calculations involving such factors as loading, fuel, endurance and take-off and landing weights, while the air electronics officer collated all the callsigns and classified codes which were to be used during the sortie. After each crew member had undergone his individual briefing, the crew would be assembled and briefed on the sortie by the captain. The aircraft would then be handed over by the crew chief and its crew would enter the cockpit to carry out their pre-flight checks, which occupied about an hour in the case of the Valiant, although in the case of an aircraft on an alert exercise this would already have been done and everything would be switched on and ready for engine start.

When a Valiant crew was called to readiness or summoned for an alert exercise, crew members reported to the

V-bomber aircrew practising a 'scramble', racing for the crew buses that will take them to their aircraft. The operational readiness technique was greatly improved as the force gained experience. *MoD (RAF)*

Operations Wing (with sufficient kit for an indefinite stay away from base) and were briefed on the nature of the sortie. Each crew would undergo the usual pre-flight briefing routine, and then all the crews would be subjected to further briefings by specialist officers; for example, the AEOs would be briefed by the Wing AEO. The crews would then go into a waiting posture while the aircraft was made combat-ready, each Valiant having to meet a stringent preparation level. When this was achieved, crews would go out to their aircraft to carry out the appropriate checks; the cockpit door would then be locked and no one allowed inside except crew members.

The crews would then await the alert call, which was sounded either by klaxon or station broadcast over the tannoy. The initial call brought them to 'Readiness One Five'

(15min) and they would remain inside the cockpit with the door locked and ground crew standing by, the aircraft crew connected by teletalk (known colloquially as the 'Bomber Box') to the Operations Controller in the Bomber Command Operations Room at RAF High Wycombe in Buckinghamshire. Over the teletalk, the crew could hear dispersal instructions being issued to other units; these usually followed a set pattern, with units being brought to five-minute readiness, followed by two-minute readiness, then scrambled. Engines were started at 'Readiness Zero Two'.

Bottom Left and Bottom Right:
On 3 July 1958, the nosewheel fell off Vulcan B1 XH497 of No 617 Squadron. The rear crew baled out, one of them unfortunately being killed when his parachute failed to open, and the pilot, Flt Lt Graham Smeaton, landed the aircraft successfully on its mainwheels and nosewheel strut at RAF Scampton. *MoD (RAF)*

Top Left:
Vulcan XA907 of No 83 Squadron in formation with RAAF Sabres and a Canberra during a visit to the Far East. *MoD (RAF)*

Above:
Vulcan B1s of No 617 Squadron and their crews at Farnborough in September 1960, where they demonstrated a scramble time of 1min 24sec. *MoD(RAF)*

After the order to scramble, squadron crews would go straight into a training profile, a cross-country flight with radar bomb scores, or be dispersed to pre-determined airfields in clutches of four aircraft. Throughout its career, the V-Force relied on dispersal, ultimately to 36 designated airfields, as a security against surprise attack; unlike SAC, it never maintained an airborne alert force. In the case of a prolonged exercise, lasting one or two weeks, the force would remain dispersed, the crews living alongside their aircraft and continually practising alert readiness checks with the Bomber Controller. A comprehensive debrief was held after each exercise, the results analysed and, if necessary, operational procedures amended. Much depended on the expertise of the crews, all of whom were vetted by AVM Cross before they went on the Valiant course. He said later:

'I must have seen some hundreds of aircrew in the process, and remarkable as it was, I hardly turned down one in the whole lot. They of course had all been selected by people who knew and they were first-class people and none of them ever had any doubts about what they were about to do.'

V-Force crews were subsequently graded into four categories: Unclassified, on first joining their squadron; Combat, Select and Select Star, each category being harder to attain until the final accolade of Select Star was reached by a few, these being the elite crews who could go anywhere at any time, arriving within seconds of their estimate to hit a target with an aiming error of only a few yards.

V-Force exercises around the United Kingdom presented a real challenge for the air defence squadrons of Fighter Command, which in 1957 were armed with Hawker Hunter F6 day-fighters and Gloster Javelin all-weather interceptors. Previously, the Hunters had been able to cope adequately with the B-47s and Canberras that were their principal exercise targets — and could certainly have coped equally well with the first-line bombers then in service with the Soviet Air Force — but the Valiant was something else. Whereas the B-47s and Canberras usually operated at between 35,000 and 43,000ft (10,675 and 13,115m) and presented few interception problems, the Valiant's operational ceiling of 49,000ft (14,945m) gave it a valuable extra margin with which to evade the attacking fighter. And the Valiant was only the beginning; the spearhead of the RAF's strategic deterrent force was gradually being forged from the squadrons then rearming with the Vulcan B1, and the last of the trio of V-bombers, the Handley Page Victor, promised a still higher performance.

The Vulcans and Victors were already appearing in exercises towards the end of 1957, and the Hunter pilots quickly found that successful interceptions of either type were extremely difficult unless the fighters had a height and speed advantage, which was not often the case; the Hunter F6 was only marginally faster at altitude than either the Vulcan or the Victor B1, and it could not match their operational ceiling of 55,000ft (16,775m). The key to a successful interception of either type was to obtain a visual sighting at long range, giving the Hunter pilot time to manoeuvre into a favourable attacking position; pilots were often helped by contrails,

which enabled sightings to be made at up to 25 miles, but with no trails visible it was rare for a sighting to be made beyond 10 miles, and in this case the interception became critical. In any case, the sighting of contrails was only of value if it enabled the Hunter to make its interception below 48,000ft (14,640m); anything over that was outside the Hunter's effective limits.[46]

As V-Force expertise grew, overseas exercises became more frequent. Squadrons would send detachments to Malaya (Exercise 'Sunflower') for up to a month, a series of local familiarisation flights being followed by a full-scale exercise with SEATO air forces. Squadron deployments were also made to Luqa, Malta (Exercise 'Sunspot'), during which crews would carry out visual bombing over the El Adem range, Libya, with practice and live HE bombs. There were also single-aircraft 'Lone Ranger' flights, mainly to El Adem, Cyprus and Nairobi; equivalent single-crew flights to Norway were known as 'Polar Bears' and those to the United States as 'Western Rangers'.

In October 1957, two Valiants — both from No 138 Squadron, but with one crew from No 214, together with two Vulcans from No 83 Squadron — represented RAF Bomber Command in the SAC annual bombing competition, held at Pinecastle AFB in Florida. It was the first time that V-Force aircraft had taken part in this competition, which lasted for six nights and involved 45 SAC bomb wings, each one represented by two aircraft and two crews, flying on three alternate nights. The route, flown as a level cruise, was more than 2,700nm (5,000km) long and included an astro-navigation leg of over 800nm (1,482km) and three widely spaced simulated bombing attacks. There were strict limitations, including a take-off 'window' of five minutes and an en route tolerance of plus or minus three minutes; failure to meet these automatically disqualified a crew, as did the failure to achieve a competition total of six scored bomb runs and two scored astro runs.

The two Valiants that took part were among the first to be delivered to the RAF with underwing fuel tanks, and were resplendent in their new white anti-flash finish. The competition began on 30 October and ended on 5 November, the RAF crews arriving three weeks early in order to familiarise themselves with SAC procedures and target data. The three targets were very precise. The first was the base of the northeast corner of the Columbian Steel Tank Company building in Kansas City; the second the centre of the turntable in the railway marshalling yards at St Louis; and the third the top of the northwest corner of the General Services warehouse in Atlanta. Despite some initial difficulty with the navigation bombing system in one of the Valiants, their final placing was 27th out of a total of 45 teams involved, one of the Valiant crews from No 214 Squadron (Sqn Ldr Ronald Payne) being placed eleventh out of a total of 90 in the individual crew scoring part of the contest. Considering the quality and quantity of the SAC crews, it was a very satisfactory result for the Valiant crews, although the Vulcans did not do so well, being placed 44th overall. Some of the Vulcans' electronic equipment was affected by the high humidity, and the bombing altitude of 36,000ft (10,980m) was well below that at which their crews had been practising. Nevertheless, Bomber

Left:
The Boeing B-47 Stratojet, which entered service in 1951, gave the Americans a considerable lead in the development of a nuclear-capable bombing fleet.
Philip Jarret Collection

Right:
A member of a Vulcan crew explains the workings of the V-bomber to some USAF ground crew during a 'Western Ranger' sortie to the USA.
AVM Ron Dick

This spread:
In October/November 1959, four Vulcan B1s of No 617 Squadron flew to Ohakea, New Zealand, to represent Bomber Command at the official opening of Wellington International Airport. The three aircraft seen in these photographs went on to complete a round-the-world trip by continuing eastwards across the Pacific to the UK via the United States. *MoD (RAF)*

Command's participation yielded some valuable lessons, and it was to be an annual event from then on, with only an occasional break for operational or technical reasons.

All these exercises provided V-Force crews with invaluable operational training under widely differing conditions, as well as having the very worthwhile secondary effect of 'showing the flag' for the Royal Air Force. Further valuable training on a competitive basis was provided by the annual Bomber Command bombing competition, which introduced a considerable element of rivalry not only between individual crews but also between the two RAF Bomber Groups, No 3 with Valiants (and Victors from 1960) and No 1 with Vulcans. The competition would last for three days, with an optional fourth day to allow for bad weather. Each participating crew

was accompanied by an umpire. The contest was very exacting, particularly for the navigators, who had to demonstrate their ability to operate using only limited equipment over a leg of about 800nm (1,482km). Astro-navigation featured prominently, the radar navigator taking celestial shots with a sextant and the navigator plotter working out headings and ETAs with the information so obtained. The leg terminated over a radar bombing site, the end-of-leg position being determined by a signal sent out from the aircraft. This was plotted on the ground and the navigation error calculated accordingly. AEOs were required to receive coded message groups within a specified time, and all the results achieved were collated to produce individual crew ratings.

Left and Bottom Left:
The fourth Vulcan on the New Zealand tour, XH498, undershot the runway at Wellington while attempting a landing, sustaining damage to the port undercarriage and fuel tank. The captain managed to overshoot and flew back to Ohakea, where he made an emergency landing.
Author's Collection

Top Right:
XH498 after repair seven months later, taking off on an air test prior to returning to the UK.
Author's Collection

Centre Right:
Vulcan B1 of No 617 Squadron, with aircrews. *Author's Collection*

Bottom Right:
Vulcan B1A XH481 of No 101 Squadron seen at Perth, Australia, after making a nonstop UK-Australia flight in 1961. *MoD (RAF)*

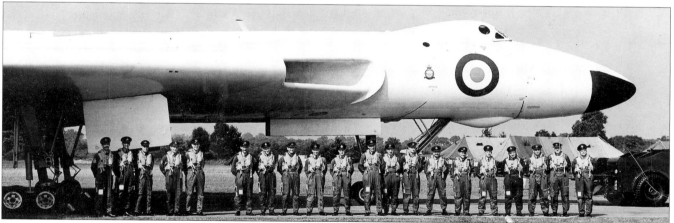

Top Left and Below Left:
Vulcan B2s of the Waddington Wing
with BAC Lightning fighters.
MoD (RAF)

Top Right and Bottom Right:
Two views of a Vulcan B2 taking off
from Scampton. *MoD (RAF)*

Above:
Vulcan B1A XH502 of the Waddington Wing. This aircraft was the last B1A at Waddington, being relegated to ground instructional duties in January 1968.
MoD (RAF)

Below:
The V-bombers: Valiants, Victors and Vulcans. The second pair of Valiants, sporting camouflage, are aircraft assigned to SACEUR.
Author's Collection

9 DEFENDING THE V-BOMBER BASES

In May 1945, of the eight Fighter Command groups which had been responsible for the air defence of the UK, only two — Nos 11 and 12 — were on full status, defending the country east and south of a line joining Cape Wrath at the northwest tip of Scotland, Banbury in Oxfordshire and St David's in Pembrokeshire. By December 1946, Fighter Command's front-line strength was 192 aircraft in 18 day-fighter squadrons, each established with eight aircraft and armed with a mixture of Vampire, Meteor and Hornet aircraft, and six night-fighter squadrons armed with Mosquitos. In addition, 20 Auxiliary squadrons, armed for the time being with piston-engined aircraft like the Spitfire and Mosquito, were in the process of re-formation.

In December 1946, an Air Staff Directive to the AOC-in-C Fighter Command ordered that the command's first priority during the next two years would be to concentrate on research and experimentation in air defence techniques, the main goals being to achieve the highest possible interception rate by day and night irrespective of the weather, to improve the raid reporting and fighter control organisation, and to standardise operational and training techniques to permit the rapid reinforcement of the command in an emergency by fighter squadrons from Germany. This directive was based on the so-called Ten-Year Rule, which for defence planning purposes assumed that no threat of a major conflict would arise for at least ten years. Maximum use was to be made of existing aircraft, equipment and weapons, most of which would not be replaced until 1957 or thereabouts. There were enormous difficulties to be faced, of which a virtually bankrupt economy was only one. From a wartime air force over a million strong, the postwar RAF was being progressively demobilised to a strength of around 300,000 all ranks; notwithstanding the reductions, manpower and aircraft still had to be spread over the whole UK commitment overseas, from Germany to the Far East.

The Air Ministry, well aware of the constraints it would have to face in the immediate postwar years, had nevertheless given much thought to the shape and organisation of the postwar air defences, as well as to the type of radars and data-processing equipment that would be required. As early as July 1945 it had issued a paper proposing a 'Defended Area' to be manned by a regular air defence force capable of expansion at short notice, and a 'Shadow Area' where a non-operational air defence network would be manned by a fully trained but non-regular reserve force; this could be brought to full

operational status within two years. The Air Ministry also envisaged that the air defences would have to cope with targets flying at 600kt (1,100km/h) at up to 100,000ft (30,500m), which meant that a future generation of early warning radars must be able to detect high-level targets at a range of 330 miles (530km) and low-level targets at about 200 miles (320km).

A new radar system would have to incorporate secure IFF (Identification Friend/Foe) and have the capability to transmit a display of the recognised air picture to command and control centres up to 1,000 miles (1,600km) away.

Fighter Command worked hard to set up the Defended Area, initially from Flamborough Head in Yorkshire to Portland Bill on the Channel, but its efforts were hampered when the government called for a rapid rundown of manpower which left only 36 radars operational. The command managed to set up four operational Master GCI (Ground-Controlled Interception) stations in time for the major air exercises that took place in the autumn of 1948, after the Berlin Crisis had developed, but even with a renewed interest in defence spending the best that could be done in the short term was to update the old wartime system by duplicating the radar cover. In the meantime — as the air exercises revealed — British targets were virtually indefensible. During Exercise 'Dagger', for example, the defending fighters recorded a kill rate of only 15% against attacking USAF B-29s.

The Berlin Crisis, and subsequent events of 1949, effectively tore the Ten-Year Rule to shreds and led to a major reassessment of future air defence policy. Production of jet interceptors would now be doubled, and reconditioning of older fighter types accelerated. Air defences were to be improved with new equipment, and the Auxiliary squadrons were to be brought up to strength and rearmed with jet aircraft as soon as possible. With the pace starting to quicken, a new Air Ministry Directive was issued to the AOC-in-C Fighter Command in August 1949, reflecting the urgency of the situation. In contrast to the previous one, which was concerned with research and experimentation in air defence and in the defence only of the area of the United Kingdom which could be manned effectively, the new directive stated firmly that the command's operational commitment was the defence of the whole United Kingdom against air attack. Plans to strengthen Fighter Command and improve its equipment were further accelerated in the autumn of 1949, for by then

the perceived threat from the Soviet Union had assumed potentially formidable proportions.

By this time, Fighter Command's day-fighter strength had been doubled and all squadrons were now equipped with jets — all of them inferior to the MiG-15, whose introduction in increasing numbers was viewed with mounting concern. Only one aircraft on the NATO inventory could meet the MiG-15 on equal terms, and the summer of 1951 saw its first deployment to Britain. It was the North American F-86 Sabre, which armed one USAF wing, one RCAF wing and two squadrons of Fighter Command in the UK.

By the beginning of 1953, the UK air defences were facing realistic opposition following the deployment in numbers of the English Electric Canberra B2 jet bomber. In May 1953, for example, Canberras of the Binbrook Wing took the part of the enemy in Exercise 'Rat/Terrier', carrying out low-level attacks on the USAF bases at Lakenheath and Sculthorpe to test the defences against this kind of strike. Earlier, on 19 March, during Exercise 'Jungle King', the Binbrook Canberras had penetrated deeply into Germany to attack the US airfields at Fürstenfeldbruck near Munich and Rhein-Main, Frankfurt. The scenario was that 45 enemy swept-wing jet fighters were refuelling at the first target and that an enemy general, in a four-engined jet transport with a 45-strong fighter escort, was calling at the second. The Canberras made a high-level GH attack and successfully completed their mission.

USAF and RCAF Sabre pilots found the Canberra a very difficult aircraft to intercept, for it was very manoeuvrable at low and medium altitudes, and at high altitudes it could outclimb the F-86. For RAF Fighter Command, armed with the Meteor F8, it was a particularly frustrating time. The diary of No 43 Squadron (RAF Leuchars, Scotland) recorded that:

'It was most disconcerting to find Canberras out-turning us at 40,000 feet and converting their mild evasive-action-only tactics into perfect quarter attacks on our exposed bottoms . . .'

Fighter Command could only eagerly await the introduction of the Hawker Hunter and Supermarine Swift, scheduled for early in 1954; even then an unforeseen disappointment was in store, for the Swift was to show characteristics that made it unacceptable as a fighter.

The early service career of the Hunter was also troubled by problems with the cannon and with the fuel system; the aircraft also had a very poor combat radius. By the end of 1956, however, Fighter Command had 16 squadrons of the improved Hunter F6 at its disposal, the policy being to concentrate and one night-fighter and two day-fighter squadrons to form a single wing on an operational airfield.

As the quality of the aircraft assigned to UK air defence improved, strenuous efforts were being made to update the warning radar system, but the best that could be done in the short term was to update the existing system by duplicating the radar cover, making some of it mobile, going underground for protection where possible, making the radars more reliable and easier to maintain and improving the readiness by deploying more manpower on watch. This led to the so-called 'Rotor' programme, in which immediate steps were taken to modify the old wartime radars pending the introduction of new ones from 1957. In fact, technological progress made it possible to begin installing the new radars by the end of 1954.

The new TRE Type 80 radar provided good long-range coverage, being able to track targets down to the horizon,

which in practice meant 22,000ft (6,700m) at 200nm (370km). However, the deployment of thermonuclear weapons in both East and West led to the concept of a short three-day war in which Britain and the RAF's retaliatory forces could not hope to survive unless high-speed, high-altitude enemy aircraft carrying H-bombs were destroyed, and in its early stages 'Rotor' could not be relied upon to give sufficient early warning.

Air defence planning in the early 1950s, designed to counter the perceived air threat to the UK in the 1960-70 period, envisaged that from about 1960 the USSR would be able to threaten the United Kingdom with medium-range (1,500nm/2,775km) ballistic missiles or with attacks by

Left:
The BAC (English Electric) Lightning was the RAF's primary air defence fighter aircraft for the V-bomber bases during the 1960s.
Ian Allan Library

Right:
The Bristol Bloodhound surface-to-air missile was deployed in defence of the V-bomber bases. It could be fitted with a nuclear warhead.
Author's Collection

medium- and high-altitude aircraft carrying free-fall and stand-off nuclear weapons and flying at increasingly faster speeds and heights — possibly 2.5M at 70,000ft (21,350m) by 1970. Low-altitude subsonic attacks could also be expected, most probably supported by intense electronic countermeasures (ECM). The defensive system to counter these threats would have to be proof against saturation by large numbers of aircraft, and the warning time had to be long enough to ensure interception at least 20 miles (32km) from the coast.

In 1957, however, with the first squadrons of the RAF's nuclear deterrent force in place, existing fighter aircraft were considered adequate to deal with the existing air threat; the Hawker Hunter F6 and the newly-deployed all-weather fighter, the Gloster Javelin, made a powerful combination. The Hunter's four 30mm Aden cannon, which could deliver 10 times as much explosive per second as, for example, the MiG-17's armament, marked the biggest advance in the fighter's weaponry since the introduction of the 20mm Hispano cannon in 1941, while the Javelin, from 1958, was armed with the Firestreak heat-seeking air-to-air missile (AAM). The Javelin had already proved that it could meet the air defence criteria; the first production aircraft, in air exercises, had successfully intercepted Canberras 100 miles (161km) from the British coast.

In January 1957 Fighter Command reached an all-time Cold War high, with 448 day-fighters in eighteen Regular and Auxiliary squadrons (the latter anticipating early re-equipment with the Hunter) and 272 night/all-weather fighters in seventeen squadrons. Then came the bombshell: the Defence White Paper of April 1957, which was to bring about a massive reduction in the UK fighter force between 1957 and 1960.

The policy at this time was to use both fighters and surface-to-air missiles in the air defence of the UK, with the national early warning radar system linked to the NATO radar system on the Continent. From April 1957, however, the concept of deterrence was to form the basis of future British defence policy, which meant that the defence of the V-bomber bases was to have the utmost priority. For this purpose, a greatly reduced fighter force was considered adequate, operating in conjunction with the first-generation Bloodhound SAM, a weapon still under development but expected to be in service by 1959. It was envisaged that SAMs would eventually replace manned fighter aircraft completely, and in these circumstances it was unlikely that the RAF would need a fighter aircraft to follow on from the English Electric Lightning, which was also expected to be in squadron service in 1959-60.

At one time, when the deployment of Thor IRBMs to the United Kingdom was first under discussion, it was thought that the USAF might also deploy advanced supersonic fighters (probably the Lockheed F-104 Starfighter) to defend both SAC and Bomber Command bases. In the event this never

happened, and it was the Lightning — essentially an experimental aircraft fitted with a weapons system — that was rushed into service. Like the F-104 Starfighter, the Lightning was developed as a supersonic missile-armed interceptor, but it had none of the Starfighter's limitations; in fact the Lightning was the world's only supersonic pure 'fighter' aircraft until the advent of the McDonnell Douglas F-15, and by the time the latter flew in prototype form the Lightning had already been in RAF service for 12 years. The Lightning, to be sure, had its fair share of problems — including an inadequate weapons system — but its ability to get off the ground very quickly and climb to 30,000ft (9,150m) in a little under two minutes were important assets in an era when it was assumed that an East-West war would begin with a nuclear attack on airfields, with minimum warning time.

The Lightning, which entered service in the summer of 1960 and was given a flight refuelling capability from the F Mk 1A onwards, remained the RAF's primary air defence system during the remaining years of the V-Force's Quick Reaction Alert (QRA) role. The other component of the system was the Bristol Bloodhound surface-to-air missile, the Mk 1 version of which began to be deployed in 1958; eventually, Bloodhounds armed 14 air defence missile squadrons in the protection of the V-bomber bases. Although integrated with the existing control and reporting network, each Bloodhound base required an intermediate radar in closer proximity than the Type 80 surveillance stations. In response to this need, Metropolitan-Vickers developed a new three-dimensional tactical radar linked to a high data-rate computer; this fed target data to the fire units, which usually comprised four sections of 16 launchers each.

Bloodhound was launched by four Bristol Aerojet solid fuel boost motors, and cruised to the target at 2.0M under ramjet power. The missile was fitted with a large conventional warhead, but a nuclear warhead ('Indigo Hammer') was also developed for possible use in the Mk 2 version, deployed from 1964. The Mk 2 used either a portable or fixed-base form; the portable system used the Ferranti Firelight target illuminating radar (TIR), while the fixed-base set employed the more powerful AEI Scorpion. The TIR was directed towards the target by surveillance radar and the reflected radar energy was used by the Bloodhound's guidance system ('Indigo Violet') to direct the missile to its target. Range was about 50nm (93km) and the Mk 2 Bloodhound had a low-level capability, being able to engage targets flying between 200ft and 65,000ft (60-19,825m).

Although the defence of the V-bomber bases was made as tight as possible, there were always some worrying vulnerabilities, not least of which was the prospect of surprise attack by enemy infiltrators. The Royal Air Force Regiment and RAF Police trained hard and constantly to deal with this kind of threat.

10 BOMBER COMMAND'S THOR MISSILES

At the end of 1958, the RAF's V-bomber force comprised 82 aircraft — 54 Valiants, 18 Vulcans and 10 Victors — in 12 squadrons. Of these, seven were armed with the Valiant, three with the Vulcan and two with the Victor. The principal nuclear weapon was the 'Blue Danube', with a very small stock of the 'Violet Club' interim high-yield weapon to provide an emergency megaton attack capability pending the introduction of the 'Yellow Sun' Mk 1.

This was a significant period, for it saw the beginning of full co-operation between the USAF SAC and RAF Bomber Command in co-ordinating atomic strike plans. This involved not only operational procedures and targeting, but also the supply of American nuclear weapons to the V-Force, a possibility that had been under discussion at ministerial level since 1954. The provision of US atomic weapons was further discussed in March 1957, when Prime Minister Harold Macmillan met President Eisenhower for talks in Bermuda, as was the deployment of American IRBMs to the UK, and in June 1958 the AOC-in-C Bomber Command, Air Chief Marshal Sir Harry Broadhurst, went to SAC HQ at Omaha to confer with the Commanding General, Thomas S. Power.

As a result of this meeting, Broadhurst was able to report to the Vice Chief of Air Staff on 25 June 1958 that the purpose of his meeting with Power had been:

'To prepare a co-ordinated nuclear strike plan, based on the target directive contained in COS(57)244 dated 16 October 1957, which could be put into effect should combined nuclear retaliation by Bomber Command and SAC ever be required. The plan, approved by C-in-C SAC and myself, is applicable to the period 1 July 1958 to 30 June 1959, is targeted to utilise stocks of British, and after October 1958 USAF, nuclear weapons for the Medium Bomber Force, and includes targets for the first Thor squadron expected to be operational in January 1959 . . .'[47]

Throughout the early 1950s, SAC had become increasingly involved in the development of missiles as a means of increasing its long-range striking power. The actual development and testing of missiles remained in the hands of the various contractors and the Air Research and Development Command (ARDC), but SAC maintained close liaison with the missile development programmes. In 1955, after President Eisenhower had placed the highest national priority on the development of ballistic missiles, Headquarters

USAF accelerated the development of several promising missile types, and on 18 November that year HQ USAF instructed SAC to work closely with the ARDC in establishing an initial operational capability (IOC) for ICBMs, after which they would be turned over to SAC for operational use.

On 18 March 1956, HQ USAF gave SAC and the ARDC the responsibility for developing an IOC with the Thor IRBM and assigned SAC the responsibility of deploying this missile to the United Kingdom and bringing it to a combat-ready status, after which it would be turned over to the Royal Air Force. In July, HQ SAC announced that the missile programme was entering the planning phase, with interest centred primarily on the Thor IRBM, the Navaho and Snark subsonic intercontinental cruise missiles, and the Atlas and Titan ICBMs. Other missiles being developed for possible use by SAC included the air-launched Goose, Rascal and Quail.[48]

On 26 November 1956, US Secretary of Defense Charles E. Wilson gave the USAF the sole responsibility for the operational deployment and control of all land-based IRBMs and ICBMs. At the same time, the US Army was made responsible for land-based surface-to-air defensive missiles and surface-to-surface tactical missiles with a range of less than 200 miles (322km). In simple terms, this meant that the US Army was debarred from operating missiles with a range greater than 200 miles (322km).

This decision was to have a profound effect on the development and eventual deployment of one very promising IRBM, the SM-78 Jupiter. Developed by the Redstone Arsenal — and specifically by a team of former German scientists under Wernher von Braun — this 1,970-mile (3,170km) range weapon was designed for Army use, and in 1955 Defense Secretary Wilson decreed that the US Navy should join the programme with a view to the development of a seagoing version. When the army was stripped of its long-range missile programme a year later, the navy lost interest in Jupiter and opted for a more attractive solid-fuel missile system which, eventually, was to result in the Polaris SLBM.

The Jupiter programme was consequently turned over to the USAF, which accepted it somewhat unwillingly, despite its advanced nature. Jupiter was the first strategic missile in the world to feature an ablative re-entry vehicle — a nose cone consisting of multiple organic layers, designed to protect the one-megaton warhead from the enormous heat generated by atmospheric re-entry. The system was first tested in September 1956, when a Jupiter-C reached an altitude of 682

Above:
There was a very close relationship between SAC and RAF Bomber Command after 1958. Captained by Squadron Leader (later Air Vice-Marshal) Ron Dick, this Vulcan of No 9 Squadron — bearing the name *Mayflower III* — flew to Hanscom AFB, Massachusetts, bearing messages of greeting from the Council of Boston, Lincolnshire, on the anniversary of the sailing of the original *Mayflower*. *AVM Ron Dick*

miles (1,097km), and tests of prototypes continued throughout 1957. By July 1958 there had been 29 total and seven partial successes out of 38 launches.[49]

The intention was to deploy Jupiter to locations in Italy and Turkey under the auspices of NATO. The missiles were to be jointly manned by Italian, Turkish and United States crews under the 'dual-key' launch system, and SAC was to be responsible for all training. For this purpose, the 864th and 865th Strategic Missile Squadrons were activated at Huntsville, Alabama — where the Redstone Arsenal was located — early in 1958, and each squadron subsequently deployed 30 Jupiter systems to Italy and Turkey. A third unit, the 866th Technical Training Squadron, remained at Huntsville to carry on the work of missile training until it was deactivated in May 1962. The European deployment of Jupiter, always played down for political reasons, was terminated in 1964.

By 1959, therefore, the USAF already had a first-rate IRBM system in Jupiter, and moreover one which had the advantage of being mobile. The irony was that in 1955, as a result of political mismanagement and the often bitter inter-service rivalry that led to the US Army, Air Force and Navy each developing its own strategic missile system, usually with a wasteful duplication of effort, the USAF was ordered to proceed with the development of an IRBM that was similar in performance and configuration to Jupiter, but with none of the latter's mobility advantage. The contract went to the Douglas Aircraft Corporation, which by prodigious feats of design and engineering delivered the first SM-75 Thor in October 1956. Despite an inauspicious start to the flight test programme — the first four launches ended in failure — the system was declared operational in 1959. The missile itself carried the same warhead over the same range as Jupiter, but unlike the latter missile it was designed for fixed-base deployment. Both Thor and Jupiter were liquid-fuelled, but because it was not mobile, Thor was far more vulnerable to surprise attack.[50]

From the beginning, it had been the intention of the United States government to deploy Thor missiles to Britain. This proposal was put forward in January 1957 to the British Defence Minister, Duncan Sandys, who was a firm advocate of ballistic missiles and was deeply involved in the development of Britain's own IRBM, Blue Streak. The latter weapon, however, was not expected to be ready for deployment for some years (in fact, it was never to be deployed at all) and the prospect of an interim deterrent in the form of Thor seemed attractive. Thor, the Americans emphasised, would cost Britain nothing except the outlay of funds necessary for site preparation, and to avoid political complications the missiles would be manned by the Royal Air Force, though the warheads would remain under American control.

Despite considerable opposition from various quarters in Britain, plans for the deployment of Thor went ahead, and in February 1958 a joint government agreement was signed. It provided for the US Third Air Force to assist in the construction of the Thor sites and deliver the missiles to the RAF, which would maintain and control them, while targeting was to be a matter of joint operational policy, relying on the close liaison already established between SAC and RAF Bomber Command. On 20 February, the 705th Strategic Missile Wing was activated at RAF Lakenheath and assigned to the 7th Air Division, moving to South Ruislip shortly afterwards to merge with the Divisional HQ. Prior to this, the 392nd Missile Training Squadron had been activated at Vandenberg AFB on 15 September 1957 for the training of RAF Thor crews.

The original plan was for four RAF Bomber Command squadrons to operate a total of 60 Thors at four specially-constructed sites, but because of the system's vulnerability and the consequent need for dispersal this was quickly revised. The Thors would now be operated by twenty squadrons, each with its own site and three missiles. After its number, each squadron would carry the initials SM (Strategic Missile) — the only RAF squadrons ever to bear this designation.

The first of the designated squadrons, No 77 (SM), was reformed at RAF Feltwell in Norfolk on 1 September 1958. As yet without missiles, its task was to establish training techniques and procedures with SAC. Prior to April 1959 the US research and production facilities had been directed mainly towards proving the Thor weapon system at White Sands, New Mexico and Cape Canaveral, Florida, and to setting up the first two missile sites in the United Kingdom. Very little equipment was dedicated to training, and it was not until 16 April 1959 that an RAF crew of No 98 (SM) Squadron, having received formal Integrated Weapon System training, became the first to launch a Thor. Royal Air Force launch crews, consisting of a General Duties officer (usually a squadron leader) as Launch Control Officer, three aircrew NCOs as Launch Control Console Operators, and three technicians as Missile Maintenance Technicians, were initially trained at the Douglas Aircraft Company school at Tucson, Arizona. Training comprised missile theory, construction and operation, and an introduction to the necessary ground support equipment. A realistic simulator was used for instruction in countdown sequences, and malfunctions could also be incorporated for emergency training. On graduating

from Tucson, the crews went to the 392nd MTS at Vandenberg AFB, where they received more detailed training using operational equipment.[51]

On 19 September 1958 No 77 (SM) Squadron received its first Thor, which was flown to RAF Feltwell aboard a C-124 Globemaster, and all subsequent missiles were delivered by this means, along with their ancillary equipment. The missile was still being operationally proven as a weapon system, however, and nearly a year was to elapse before the next batch of RAF squadrons was declared operational with the Thor in July 1959. All 20 squadrons were operational by the end of the year.

The three missiles at each site were not readily visible to the casual onlooker. For much of the time they lay prone and invisible in their shelters, behind heavily guarded perimeters, being erected only for practice countdowns. Any launch order, simulated or otherwise, had to be authenticated by RAF and USAF officers at HQ Bomber Command and HQ 7th Air Division, using a special and highly secret code. Operation of the Thor required a lengthy countdown procedure, so in time of crisis the system required plenty of warning of impending hostile activity; on average, the sequence required something like 105 minutes from receipt of the positive launch order. At that point the RAF Launch Control Officer turned a phase sequence key to initiate a fully automatic sequence of events: the guidance system was aligned and checked, the shelter moved back and the missile raised slowly to the upright position, while the liquid propellants were pumped into the missile at a high rate. They had to be pumped out again after a simulated launch, because the Thor could remain fuelled only for a limited period before it had to be stood down.

The liquid-fuel rocket motor was the Thor's principal disadvantage, but there were others. Further time would have been needed to fit the nuclear warheads, which were not kept on site but stored with other nuclear weaponry under extreme security at Faldingworth, an old wartime airfield near Scampton, Lincolnshire. Such was the secrecy surrounding Faldingworth that from 1957 to 1980 the airfield was not shown on Ordnance Survey maps. Spare parts for the Thors in the UK were held in the United States; RAF squadron supply officers could indent directly for spares by radio link and receive them immediately by air, as all equipment could be carried in the C-124 Globemaster.

The Thor deployment to the United Kingdom was nothing more than an interim measure, designed to plug a dangerous gap until SAC's ICBM force became fully operational, but it undoubtedly had a valuable deterrent effect during the dangerous crisis that developed in October 1962, when the Americans discovered that Soviet missiles and jet bombers were clandestinely being supplied to Cuba. The response to this crisis was very much an American affair, but it is worth examining in some detail, as the RAF did have a part to play.

Both CIA and Air Force U-2 high-altitude reconnaissance aircraft had been monitoring Cuba ever since 1959, when

Fidel Castro had become premier after overthrowing the pro-American government of President Batista. On 29 August 1962, a CIA U-2 returned with photographic evidence that SA-2 'Guideline' SAM sites were being built on the island. The presence of Soviet-built MiG-21 interceptors on Cuban airfields had already been noted, and at first sight it might have been thought that the SA-2s were merely the second component of a newer and modern air defence system being installed by the Soviets. But SA-2 sites had been photographed in the Soviet Union, and the CIA photo interpreters knew that they followed set patterns, depending on the kind of target they were designed to defend. For example, SA-2 sites in the shape of a trapezoid were designed to protect nuclear weapons storage bunkers, medium- and intermediate-range ballistic missile complexes, shipyards and bomber bases. The SAM sites being set up in Cuba were in the form of a trapezoid.

As the weeks went by, the evidence began to accumulate that the Soviets were up to something in Cuba. Soviet freighters heading from the Black Sea to Havana carried mysterious crates that might contain Ilyushin Il-28 jet bombers or even strategic missiles. Armed with this alarming information, President John F. Kennedy ordered the overflights to be stepped up, although each one must have presidential approval. The flights were also to be conducted by SAC pilots, rather than CIA; the thinking was that if a U-2 were to be shot down over Cuba during any forthcoming hostilities, its pilot would be treated as a legitimate prisoner of war.

On Sunday, 14 October 1962, two U-2s of the 4080th Strategic Reconnaissance Wing took off from McCoy AFB in Florida and headed for Cuba. The U-2s were assigned different sectors, and it was the aircraft photographing the San Cristobal area which came back with the evidence that proved beyond all doubt that the Soviets were preparing to deploy medium- and intermediate-range ballistic missiles to Cuba. The photographs revealed missile transporters, erector-launchers, control bunkers, vehicle revetments, oxidizer and propellant trucks, tented and prefabricated accommodation, and large mounds of earth that clearly concealed nuclear warhead storage bunkers.

The missiles were identified as the SS-4 'Sandal' MRBM, which had a range of around 1,250 miles (2,012km) and was the first Soviet missile to use storable liquid fuel. The IRBM was the SS-5 'Skean', which had a range of around 2,000 miles (3,218km). Both missiles had their drawbacks in operational use, their launch process involving an enormous amount of time and effort. The SS-4 needed about eight hours' preparation time before firing, and the SS-5 could be maintained at a state of readiness for only five hours.

The air reconnaissance effort over Cuba was dramatically intensified, the U-2s of the 4080th SRW overflying the island 102 times between 14 October and 16 December 1962. Low-level reconnaissance sorties over Cuba were also made by RF-101 Voodoos of the 363rd Tactical Reconnaissance Wing from Shaw AFB in South Carolina and by RF-8A Crusaders of the US Navy's Light Photographic Squadron 26. Three U-2s were lost during these operations. One of them, flown by Major Rudolf Anderson, was shot down over the naval base at Banes by an SA-2 missile on 27 October and its pilot killed; the others disappeared in unknown circumstances.

At 19.00 hours eastern standard time on 22 October, President Kennedy, in a televised speech lasting 17 minutes, announced to an unsuspecting American public the discovery of Soviet missiles in Cuba and the immediate imposition of a naval blockade around the island. As the President began to speak, American forces worldwide were placed on a higher state of alert, with SAC moving to Defense Condition (DEFCON) Three. Battle staffs were placed on 24-hour alert duty, leave cancelled and personnel recalled. B-47s were dispersed to several widely separated and pre-selected civilian and military airfields, additional bombers and tankers were placed on ground alert, and the B-52 airborne alert indoctrination programme was immediately expanded into an actual airborne alert involving 24-hour sorties by armed aircraft and the immediate replacement in the air of each aircraft that landed. SAC's ICBM force, at that time numbering about 200 operational missiles, was brought into alert configuration.

As the crisis developed, the US intelligence agencies believed they had identified 24 SS-4 launchers, of which twenty were fully operational; the remaining four were expected to be operational early in November. The photographic interpreters had positively identified 33 SS-4 missiles at San Cristobal and Sagua la Grande, but were of the opinion that there were probably more, while a third site at Guanajay, north of San Cristobal, was apparently being readied to receive SS-5s. The first four SS-5 launchers were expected to be operational by 1 December, and the second and third SS-5 groups by the 15th. A fourth SS-5 group was clearly planned and construction of the site had begun. In fact, delivery of the last six SS-4s (of which there were actually 42 planned for deployment) and all 32 SS-5s was blocked by the naval quarantine. No MRBM or IRBM nuclear warheads were ever identified in Cuba, but a Soviet artillery battalion equipped with Frog tactical rockets was present on the island, and it was revealed many years later that the missiles were nuclear-tipped and that its commander had the discretion to use them in the event of an American invasion.

Had war come, the spearhead of an attack on the Soviet facilities in Cuba would have been the Republic F-105 Thunderchiefs of Tactical Air Command's 4th Tactical Fighter Wing, which deployed to McCoy AFB on 21 October. The 4th TFW began a one hour alert status at 04.00 the next day, and this was reduced to 15 minutes in the afternoon. But the F-105s were held back while international negotiations proceeded, and when they flew it was in the air defence role, patrolling the southern Florida peninsula on the lookout for Il-28 jet bombers. Nevertheless, TAC's RF-101 sorties made certain that the fighter-bombers' target folders were kept updated on a regular basis. In Europe, which would certainly have been the first to feel an armed Soviet backlash against any American action in Cuba, the nuclear alert force comprised USAF F-100 Super Sabre tactical fighter bombers deployed on British bases, backed up by the Thor IRBMS deployed with the RAF in the United Kingdom, and RAF Valiant bombers armed with tactical nuclear weapons of American origin. The role of the RAF's V-bombers in the Cuban crisis will be examined in the next chapter. As far as the Thors were concerned, the plan called for the UK-based F-100s, armed with 1.1mT tactical nuclear weapons, to deliver the primary nuclear strike, which would be followed within a minute by a Thor warhead. Two Thors were targeted on East Berlin, which was regarded as one of the Warsaw Pact's principal command and control centres, and in this case a hapless F-100 pilot had the task of delivering his nuclear weapon between the explosions of the two missile warheads in order to make sure of destroying a key command bunker.

By the morning of 24 October a formidable naval blockading force was in place on the approaches to Cuba. At its heart was Task Force 136, comprising 17 destroyers, two cruisers, the attack carriers Enterprise and Independence and the antisubmarine carriers Randolph and Essex. In all, 480 ships were involved in the operation. A quarantine arc was established 500 miles northeast of Cuba and US Navy surveillance aircraft, both carrier- and shore-based, ensured that nothing entered it without being detected. When a ship was detected it was stopped, allowed to proceed if its cargo was innocuous, and turned back if it was not.

On 25 October, with no sign of an easing of tension, American forces worldwide went to DEFCON Two. At this point the Thors were at Phase 2 of the Bomber Command missile alert procedure, the missile shelters having been retracted, the missiles erected into the firing position, and target data programmed into the system. However, there is some evidence that part of the Thor force, at RAF Hemswell, were fully fuelled and at Phase 4 alert, on four minutes' readiness, with the crews' shifts extended from eight to twelve hours and the missiles being constantly topped up with liquid oxygen.

On 27 October (a Saturday) there was an indication that the RAF was about to become involved in the quarantine when Nos 42, 201 and 206 Squadrons, RAF Coastal Command at St Mawgan in Cornwall, were alerted for a deployment to the Caribbean. All three squadrons, which were armed with the Avro Shackleton and had an offensive antisubmarine role, were ready to deploy to Bermuda when their mission was cancelled at the last moment. The exact nature of that mission is still not clear, but in a report on the deployment and status of forces during the Cuban Missile Crisis, the US Joint Chiefs of Staff stated that:

'Aircraft from Bermuda and Roosevelt Roads, Puerto Rico, will conduct daylight searches to the East of the Quarantine Arc. Additional land-based patrol aircraft are being provided by COMASWFORLANT (Commander,

Antisubmarine Warfare Force, Atlantic) from Bermuda and Roosevelt Roads.'

As Bermuda was a dependent British colony, this statement implied that either the UK government had given permission for the use of its airfields by US forces, or that British maritime aircraft were taking an active part in the quarantine.

On 28 October, Premier Khrushchev agreed to the withdrawal of all offensive missiles from Cuba, subject to verification by the United Nations. It was the first major break in the crisis. Throughout the next few days, SAC reconnaissance aircraft — U-2s and RB-47s — maintained close aerial surveillance while the missiles were dismantled, loaded on ships, and sent back through the quarantine to the USSR.

On 20 November, when the Soviets agreed to move their Il-28 medium bombers from Cuba, the quarantine was lifted and the air and naval forces began shifting back to normal operations. In SAC, the B-47 medium bombers returned to their home bases, the ground alert force dropped back to the normal 50% standard, and routine B-52 airborne alert indoctrination flights recommenced.

The Cuban crisis was a unique example of Anglo-American co-operation at the highest strategic level. It also demonstrated the ability of the RAF to generate all its nuclear strike forces at short notice, the fruit of several years of constant practice and realistic training. It came almost at the end of the Thor's operational deployment with Bomber Command; the Thor operation began to wind down early in 1963 and was terminated by the end of that year, the RAF having cancelled its combat training launches at Vandenberg in August 1962.

The RAF's Thor Squadrons and their Bases

Sqn	Base	Period of Deployment
77	Feltwell	September 1958-July 1963
82	Shepherds Grove	July 1959-July 1963
97	Hemswell	July 1959-May 1963
98	Driffield	November 1959-June 1963
102	Full Sutton	November 1959-April 1963
104	Ludford Magna	July 1959-May 1963
106	Bardney	July 1959-May 1963
107	Tuddenham	September 1959-July 1963
113	Mepal	July 1959-July 1963
130	Polebrook	December 1959-August 1963
142	Coleby Grange	September 1959-May 1963
144	North Luffenham	February 1960-August 1963
150	Carnaby	August 1959-April 1963
218	Harrington	December 1959-August 1963
220	North Pickenham	July 1959-July 1963
223	Folkingham	February 1960-August 1963
226	Catfoss	November 1959-March 1963
240	Breighton	August 1959-January 1963
254	Melton Mowbray	December 1959-February 1963
269	Caistor	September 1959-May 1963

11 THE MK 2 V-BOMBERS & STAND-OFF WEAPONS

Despite the restrictions of the US Atomic Energy Act (the McMahon Act) which vetoed the release of information on nuclear research to foreign powers — which, of course, included Britain — an extremely close relationship continued to exist between the RAF and USAF in the immediate postwar years. After all, the two Services had fought alongside one another in most theatres of war, and many senior officers on both sides were old comrades-in-arms. The 'special relationship' became even stronger with the re-establishment of USAF bases in the United Kingdom at the time of the Berlin crisis of 1948. Co-operation at a conventional level was further strengthened with the formation of NATO in 1949.

In one significant area, however — atomic weapons and their role within the US Strategic Air Plan — there was no

formal contact, although there may have been some at personal level on an 'old boy' basis. Throughout the late 1940s and early 1950s, the British government constantly sought to re-establish the spirit of wartime collaboration and to gain a greater degree of participation within the American nuclear programme, while at the same time pursuing its policy of developing an independent nuclear deterrent force. The approach eventually brought success; in 1952, Prime Minister Winston Churchill was given a personal briefing on the US Strategic Air Plan, and as a result of this Air Chief Marshal Sir William Dickson, the then Chief of Air Staff, was able to begin discussions with the US Air Staff on the planning requirements for an atomic counter-attack on the Soviet Air Force's long-range bomber bases in the event of general war. [52]

Further steps in strengthening the Anglo-American nuclear relationship were taken in 1954, when the US Congress approved amendments to the Atomic Energy Act which

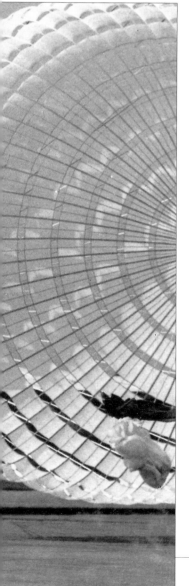

Left:
Vulcan B2 XL361 of No 617 Squadron streams its braking parachute. In December 1981, this aircraft was badly damaged at Goose Bay, Labrador, and was abandoned. *MoD (RAF)*

permitted the exchange of data on nuclear weapons in terms of size, weight, shape, yield and effects; and in 1956, when American and British observers were invited to take part as observers in one another's nuclear tests. By December 1956, it was becoming clear to the Americans that RAF Bomber Command had an increasingly viable nuclear attack force through the combination of the Valiant and 'Blue Danube', and in that month ACM Sir Dermot Boyle, now Chief of Air Staff, received proposals from General Nathan F. Twining, the USAF Chief of Staff, to provide the RAF with nuclear weapons in the event of general war and to co-ordinate the nuclear strike plans of the USAF and RAF. These proposals were later ratified in an exchange of letters between the British Minister of Defence, Duncan Sandys, and the American Secretary of Defense, Charles E. Wilson, during a meeting held in January 1957. [53]

Subsequently, in November 1957, a series of meetings between representatives of SAC and Bomber Command, with the aim of establishing a combined strike plan, revealed that all Bomber Command's targets were also covered by SAC. In the early days, following the introduction of 'Blue Danube', the RAF Medium Bomber Force had been primarily concerned with attacking targets that presented a direct offensive threat to the UK and western Europe: in other words, Soviet bomber and naval bases. Following the 1957 consultations, it was decided that the total strategic air forces at the Allies' disposal were sufficient to cover all Soviet targets, including airfields and air defence systems. On the assumption that Bomber Command's assets would be 92 aircraft by October 1958, rising to 108 aircraft by June 1959, the Command was allocated as its targets 69 cities which were centres of government or had other military significance, seventeen long-range air force airfields which formed part of the Soviet nuclear threat, and twenty elements of the Soviet air defence system. In the event of the UK being forced to take unilateral action against the Soviet Union, the target policy of Bomber Command would be to attack centres of administration and population, which was seen as the most effective system for the Command's limited resources.

In 1958, the unilateral action plan was revised to include 98 Soviet cities, all of which had a population exceeding 100,000 and which lay within 2,100nm (3,091km) of the UK. This meant, in effect, that from its earlier policy of selective attacks on military targets, Bomber Command had reverted to its wartime policy of area bombing.

The supply of US nuclear weapons to the RAF, known as Project 'E', initially involved the provision of enough 6,000lb (3,258kg) Mk 5 free-fall atomic bombs to arm 72 aircraft at Honington, Marham and Waddington. Some modifications were necessary to permit the carriage of the American weapon, but the scheme was in place by 1 October 1958, the date when the first fully co-ordinated strike plan was implemented. It caused complications in so far as the warheads themselves had to remain in American custody at the principal bases or in secure storage depots, which meant

Facing page and above:
Vulcan B2s of the Coningsby Wing — Nos 9, 12 and 35 Squadrons —
formate over the Lincolnshire countryside in a flypast to mark the station
being granted the Freedom of Boston, its home town, in 1963. *MoD (RAF)*

that they could not be flown to the V-Force dispersal airfields
in time of emergency and that there was no guarantee that the
Americans would release the weapons in time for the
V-bombers to get airborne; moreover, British nuclear
weapons could not be stored in secure storage areas occupied
by their American counterparts. There was little alternative,
however, but to continue with Project 'E' until such time as
British weapons became available in sufficient quantity to
allow the phasing out of the 'E' weapons.

In the event, project 'E' weapons were to remain on the
Bomber Command inventory until early 1963, and with the
Command's nuclear strike Canberra squadrons in Germany
until 1969. The Canberras used the 1,650lb (747kg) Mk 7.
Other American weapons assigned to Bomber Command, for
use principally by the Valiant, were the Mk 15/39 multi-
megaton bomb (7,500lb/3,397kg), reducing to 6,700lb
(3,035kg) and 6,600lb (2,989kg) in subsequent modifications;
the Mk 28 (1,900lb/860kg) and the Mk 43 (2,100lb/950kg).[54]

The definitive British free-fall megaton weapon, 'Yellow
Sun' Mk 2, was to be carried by the Mk 2 versions of the
Vulcan and Victor, the former expected to enter service in
1960. The concept of the Vulcan B2 dated to the middle of
1955, when Avro's Project Department came to the conclusion
that the existing Mk 1 airframe was capable of considerable
further development, with particular regard to the installation
of new engines, electronics and weaponry. The first task was

to create yet another change in the wing planform which, in
conjunction with increased power, would provide increased
G values, extra lift and an improved high-altitude
performance. Design of the advanced Vulcan was therefore
initiated in November 1955, and conversion of Vulcan B1
VX777 (the second prototype) as the prototype B2 was begun
in August the following year, a production order having been
placed by the Air Ministry in June.

The first pre-production Vulcan B2, XH533, flew for the first
time at Woodford on 19 August 1958, powered by Olympus
Series 200 engines. The second B2, XH534, flew in 1959,
powered by 17,000lb st Olympus 201 engines; this was the
first aircraft to be fitted with a bulged tail-cone housing ECM
equipment and tail warning radar, a feature that was to
become standard on all subsequent Vulcans. The first
example of the Vulcan B2 to be delivered to No 230 OCU,
XH558, arrived at RAF Waddington on 1 July 1960 and the first
squadron to become operational with the B2 was No 83; as
its crews returned from conversion with No 230 OCU its eight
B1s were reassigned to No 44 Squadron at Waddington from
23 December 1960.

Meanwhile, work had been proceeding at Radlett on the
design of the Victor B2. The major design change was the
installation of a new powerplant, the 17,250lb st Rolls-Royce
Conway RCo11 engine, which would give the B2 the
necessary altitude to survive in a hostile SAM environment
and ultimately provide greater range for the developing air-to-
surface missile role and also for strategic reconnaissance,
where a combination of range and altitude was necessary for
adequate coverage of potentially hostile areas. Handley Page

received a contract for 21 Victor B2s in June 1956, and following extensive ground testing of the new engines the whole of the wing root area was redesigned, with the engine bays and intakes deepened and widened. Provision was also made for the installation of a Blackburn Artouste auxiliary power unit in the starboard wing root, so that the engines could be started independently of ground services. The first Victor B2, XH668, flew for the first time on 20 February 1959, and was all set for delivery to A&AEE Boscombe Down for service handling trials when, on 20 August, it failed to return from a sortie over the Irish Sea off Pembrokeshire. The loss of the aircraft was, at the time, a complete mystery, for the impact had not been registered on radar and there had been no radio transmission from the crew. The wreckage was located and recovered for reconstruction at RAE Farnborough,

where it was eventually established that the cause of the accident had been the loss of a pitot tube, producing faulty ASI and Machmeter readings which led to the Victor exceeding its airframe limitations, going into an uncontrollable dive and breaking up. The test programme continued with the next four B2s, XH669-XH672.

The provision of effective electronic countermeasures (ECM) equipment was a major requirement for the B2 versions of the V-bombers, as will be seen in the next chapter. The B1 versions, retrofitted with new ECM, were redesignated B1A.[55]

The arming of the V-Force with stand-off weapons had been under active consideration since 1946, when the Air Staff had stated a requirement for a guided bomb. Work on this project — OR1059 Blue Boar — was undertaken by Vickers-Armstrong at Weybridge, and in 1949 drawings were produced of a TV-guided bomb designed for internal stowage, with flip-out wings, capable of being launched at altitudes of up to 60,000ft (18,300m) and at speeds of up to 600kt (1,100km/h). The TV guidance system, however, was not to the Air Staff's liking, and in June 1954 Blue Boar was cancelled in favour of the development of an inertially guided stand-off weapon with a range of 100nm (185km) and carrying an atomic warhead. An Operational Requirement for this weapon, OR1132, was issued on 3 September 1954.

Meanwhile, in 1951, there had been strong intelligence indications (which turned out to be unfounded) that the Soviet Union was on the point of carrying out some kind of military operation against the West, probably in 1953, and Winston Churchill, heading a new Conservative government, ordered a complete reappraisal of all Britain's defence capabilities. As far as Bomber Command was concerned, the position was serious; the Medium Bomber Force was still armed mainly with the Lincoln and Washington, with the Canberra just entering service, and, with the Valiant's IOC at least four years away, the Command had little in the way of offensive capability.

As a stopgap measure, two companies, Bristol and Vickers-Armstrongs, were invited to submit proposals for an unmanned flying bomb design in April 1951. The specification (UB109T) required a weapon that could be launched from a ramp and carry a 5,000lb (2,265kg) warhead at 450kt (834km/h) and 45,000ft (13,725m) over a range of 400nm (740km) — just enough to enable it to hit targets in East Germany from sites in the United Kingdom.

The design submitted by Bristol, the Type 182 Blue Rapier, was built entirely of plastic apart from the steel wing spar, and was intended for cheap mass production. It had a span of 20ft 10in (6.4m) and a length of 33ft 10in (10.4m), and all-up weight was 9,500lb (4,300kg). It had a swept wing and a small delta tailplane mounted on a stubby fin. Launching was to be achieved by means of a steam catapult, the missile cruising to its target under the power of a turbojet mounted under the fuselage. Estimated maximum speed was 550kt (1,019km/h), and Bristol estimated that each round would cost only £600. Tentative Ministry of Supply plans called for a production run of 20,000 rounds, and the weapon was intended to be barrage-launched. Two prototypes were ordered under the designation Bristol 182R; these were to be made of aluminium, equipped with Armstrong Siddeley Viper turbojets and fitted with undercarriages cannibalised from de Havilland Venom fighters.

The Vickers design to UB109T was known as Red Rapier and was built in light alloy, having three Rolls-Royce Soar expendable turbojets mounted on fuselage outriggers. Like Bristol, Vickers began construction of a prototype, but both companies abandoned the project when UB109T was cancelled in 1953. From now on, the emphasis would be on

getting the V-bombers into service as quickly as possible, and equipping them with a stand-off missile to enhance their survival chances.[56]

Following the issue of OR1132 in September 1954, both the RAE and Avro initiated studies on the feasibility of the stand-off bomb concept. By the end of 1955 most of the decisions about the missile's aerodynamics had been taken: the first was that it was to have a tail-first configuration, because this had a favourable centre of pressure change with Mach numbers; although the centre of pressure moved rearwards through the transonic regime it then moved forwards again, so that by careful design the static margin could be very nearly the same at both subsonic and supersonic speeds. This was a crucial point, for any instability during the launch phase could have serious consequences for the parent aircraft. The wing planform — a 60-degree delta — was selected because it gave good performance at transonic speed and also at the low supersonic speed that would be attained when the missile climbed. The missile was also to have two fins, an upper and lower, similar in planform to the main wing and the foreplane.

Nine models, ranging in scale from 1/6th to 1/48th, were built and subjected to wind tunnel tests, the wind tunnel programme being supplemented by a series of flight trials using 1/8th scale models. These were ground-launched, using tandem solid fuel rocket boosters.

The guidance and control system developed for the missile, known as Blue Steel from March 1956, when Avro received a development contract, consisted of three parts: the inertial navigator, designed by the RAE and supplied by Elliott Automation, and the flight rules computer and autopilot, both supplied by Avro. The decision, taken in 1954, to incorporate an inertial navigation system in the weapon, showed considerable forward thinking, for it was the only system that enabled a weapon of the Blue Steel type to navigate precisely without help from the ground and without sending out radar emissions. The general principle was that the inertial navigator computed the present position of the missile, the flight rules computer determined its flight plan, and the autopilot signalled the necessary control movements to obtain the required flight path.

During the flight prior to release, the missile's navigation system was linked with that of the parent aircraft, providing additional information to the crew on their position and, by comparing data obtained from fixes along the route, enabling corrections to be fed into the missile. The navigation system also contained a homing computer which analysed information about the missile's present position and velocity and computed the steering signals that were necessary to bring Blue Steel to its target.

Airborne trials using 2/5th scale models of Blue Steel were started in 1957, using a Valiant aircraft (WP204) based at the Avro Weapons Research Division, Woodford, the drops being made over the Aberporth range. Trials of full-size Blue Steel test vehicles began in 1958, by which time the Valiant had been joined by Vulcan XA903. The main difference between

the test vehicles and the operational Blue Steel was that the former were all powered by de Havilland Double Spectre rocket motors, whereas the operational version was to be fitted with the Armstrong (later Bristol) Siddeley Stentor. Several powered launches were made in 1959 and 1960, both at Aberporth and at Woomera in Australia. Trials with full-scale, stainless steel Stentor-powered Blue Steel trials were begun at Woomera in the summer of 1960, using Vulcans XA903 and XH539, and at a later date a Victor B2 also joined the trials programme. The Stentor motor was a dual-chamber liquid-propellant rocket engine, using kerosene as fuel and hydrogen peroxide as oxidant. Both combustion chambers fired when the missile was being boosted to supersonic speed, then the larger chamber was cut off by command from the flight rules computer. The smaller ran at full thrust for most of the climb, when it was throttled back for cruise by the flight rules computer.

The operational version of Blue Steel was 35ft (10.6m) long. Its typical range was 100nm (185km), it could be launched from both high and low level, and it attained a maximum speed of 2.5M. Its warhead was the megaton range Red Snow which was also fitted to the Yellow Sun Mk 2. A typical Blue

Steel flight profile after launch at 50,000ft (15,250m) would involve the missile climbing to 70,000ft (21,350m), followed by a sustained flight lasting about four minutes, when the missile would enter a long dive on to its target, 100nm (185km) from the launch point. There were variations to this profile; for example, Blue Steel's trajectory could be varied to give it a range of up to 200nm (370km) at a maximum speed of 1.6M, followed by a subsonic (0.8M) dive on to its target. With this profile, a Blue Steel launched over the Baltic could have destroyed Leningrad, which makes one realise how viable the missile was.[57]

The first Vulcan squadron to arm with Blue Steel was No 617 at Scampton, in the late summer of 1962. By the beginning of October the squadron had achieved an emergency IOC with the weapon, and would doubtless have used it had the Cuban missile crisis flared into war, but it was not declared fully operational until February 1963, somewhat later than planned. Later in 1963, the other squadrons of the Scampton Wing, Nos 27 and 83 Squadrons, also rearmed with Blue Steel, and the weapon's Service deployment was completed when two of No 3 Group's Victor B2 squadrons, Nos 139 and 100, followed suit at Wittering from the summer of 1963.

The Blue Steel squadrons formed the spearhead of Bomber Command's Quick Reaction Alert force, and were to do so for a further five years. QRA was inaugurated in February 1962, and the original procedure involved one aircraft from each V-Force squadron being maintained in an armed condition. Later, Operational Readiness Platforms were constructed at the ends of runways, the aircraft on readiness being parked combat-ready on short strips angled into the runway to facilitate rapid take-off. Scramble time was further reduced when, in 1962, an RAF engineer officer developed a mass

Left:
End of a Vulcan: on 6 April 1967, Vulcan B2 XL385, carrying a Blue Steel training round, was completely destroyed by fire at RAF Scampton. Five crew and one air cadet passenger escaped unhurt.
Author's Collection

Below:
Arrival of the first Blue Steel Victor Mk 2 at RAF Wittering for delivery to No 139 Squadron, August 1963.
Author's Collection

Top Right:
A Blue Steel Victor of No 100 Squadron makes a fast pass along the crowd line at RAF Wittering.
Author's Collection

Bottom Right:
SACEUR-assigned Valiants on the Operational Readiness Platform (ORP) at RAF Marham, Norfolk.
MoD (RAF)

rapid start technique, enabling all four engines of a V-bomber to be started simultaneously. With mass rapid start, four Vulcans on QRA could be airborne within 90 seconds of starting to roll.

In its early years, the V-Force relied on dispersing its aircraft to airfields all over the United Kingdom to escape the effects of enemy attack on its main bases. There were 36 such dispersal airfields in the late 1950s, reduced to 26 by 1962. These were Lossiemouth, Kinloss, Leuchars, Prestwick and Machrihanish in Scotland; Aldergrove in Northern Ireland; Middleton St George (now Teesside Airport) in County Durham; Leeming, Elvington and Leconfield in Yorkshire; Burtonwood near Manchester; Cranwell in Lincolnshire; Shawbury in Shropshire; Valley in Anglesey; Llanbedr and Brawdy in Wales; Bedford; Pershore, near Worcester; Kemble; Filton, near Bristol; Lyneham and Boscombe Down in Wiltshire; Manston in Kent; Yeovilton; Tarrant Rushton; and finally St Mawgan in Cornwall.

In 1962, with six years of experience behind it, the V-Force had become an extremely efficient organisation, with a strong nucleus of Select Star crews. Crews were assigned to QRA on a one-a-week basis, plus one weekend in every three. For the most part, there was little to do except read or play cards, the crews living in their QRA caravans beside the 'Bomber Box', the teletalk system connecting the crew to the Bomber Controller in the Bomber Command Operations Room at RAF High Wycombe, or at readiness in the cockpit depending on the alert state. In the latter case, once a scramble had been ordered all the pilot had to do was to press the mass rapid

Left:
Vulcan B2 XM574 was originally a No 27 Squadron aircraft. *MoD (RAF)*

Below:
An unusual view of a No 35 Squadron Vulcan B2A. *MoD (RAF)*

start button and everything else happened automatically, the engines lighting up and the aircraft starting to move off the operational readiness platform. The cockpits of the V-bombers were fitted with shields for protection against nuclear flash; only the forward vision panels were exposed during take-off and initial climb. During the remainder of the sortie the whole of the cockpit was blacked out, the route being flown by radar.[58]

The V-Force's efficiency was kept at a sharp edge by frequent war simulation and dispersal exercises. Exercise 'Mick', for example, involved practising alert and arming procedures without dispersing the aircraft; a no-notice exercise, it required all bomber airfields to generate — in other words, prepare for war operations — all available aircraft, bringing together the three elements of each weapons system: aircraft, weapons and aircrew. 'Kinsman' was a squadron dispersal exercise and 'Mayflight' an exercise in which all aspects of the Bomber Command dispersal and readiness plan were practised; and 'Micky Finn' was a no-notice dispersal exercise that could happen at any time of the day or night. Generating and mobilising all available aircraft and crews of a V-Force wing was a complex business, relying on up-to-date information on the movements and whereabouts of all personnel so that they could be called in, and the close control of all engineering activities so that

aircraft and weapons could be quickly recovered and brought into the line. Some aircraft would inevitably be involved in major servicing or overseas deployments; nevertheless, most of the wing's aircraft establishment — say 16 or 18 aircraft — could be generated in 10 or 12 hours.

Bomber Command was already involved in a 'Mick' exercise on 25 October 1962, when it was informed that SAC had raised its alert status to DEFCON Two in connection with the Cuban crisis. This may have been a coincidence, but it is far more likely that HQ Bomber Command had been advised by HQ SAC that something was about to happen. In any event, on 26 October the exercise was extended and the readiness state of the V-Force increased to Alert Condition 3 of the Bomber Command Alert and Readiness Procedures (Aircraft); all civilians employed on the bomber airfields were sent home, and armed patrols doubled on the airfield perimeters. Instead of generating all available aircraft, however, HQ Bomber Command ordered stations to double the number of aircraft on QRA, so that most stations had six fully armed bombers at 15 minutes' readiness. The exception was RAF Waddington, where nine fully armed Vulcans were brought to 15 minutes' readiness. The decision to generate only part of the Medium Bomber Force was almost certainly political; generating the whole of the force might have persuaded the Soviets that a pre-emptive nuclear strike was in the offing, with potentially disastrous consequences.

The Cuban crisis was evidence of the extremely high level of co-ordination and co-operation that existed between SAC and Bomber Command. Only a year earlier, in October 1961, Bomber Command had been invited to participate in Exercise 'Skyshield', designed to test the efficiency of the North American Air Defense Command (NORAD), with its early warning radar chains backed up by squadrons of long-range interceptors and surface-to-air missiles. Eight Vulcan B2s of the Scampton Wing — four from No 27 Squadron and four from No 82 — were detailed to take part in 'Skyshield', which involved a series of saturation attacks on the US air defences by SAC bombers acting as hostiles. The four No 83 Squadron aircraft went to RAF Lossiemouth in Scotland to attack with the northern wave, while the 27 Squadron Vulcans deployed

to Kindley AFB, Bermuda, to make their attack from the south. All ECM systems were to be used in the bid to break through the tight screen of USAF (and, in the northern case, RCAF) interceptors: F-101 Voodoos, F-102 Delta Daggers and Avro Canada CF-100s. The simulated attacks took place on 14 October, the Vulcans in each case preceded by USAF bombers. The northern wave was led by B-47 Stratojets, flying at low level and jamming; next came B-52s, flying between 35,000 and 42,000ft (10,675 and 12,810m), with ECM-equipped Martin RB-57s carrying out diversions; and finally, at 56,00ft (17,080m), the four 83 Squadron Vulcans, coming in singly with an interval of several minutes between each aircraft. Predictably, the fighter defences concentrated on the B-47s and B-52s, and by the time the Vulcans penetrated North American air space the defenders did not have sufficient fuel remaining to climb to their altitude. The lead Vulcan reported picking up a transmission from an F-101's fire control radar, but the other three detected nothing hostile and all four aircraft came through to land at Stephenville, Newfoundland.

The southern attack followed much the same pattern, except that in this case the four No 27 Squadron Vulcans made their penetration on a broad front, instead of in stream. Fifty miles from the coast, with fighters being launched to intercept from bases all along the eastern seaboard, the southernmost Vulcan suddenly turned north, leaving the other three to run the gauntlet of the interceptors and, at the same time, to provide a jamming screen to shield the lone aircraft. The northbound Vulcan flew parallel to the coast, then turned in to land at Plattsburgh AFB, New York, its approach completely undetected. The other three Vulcans reported intercepts, but took appropriate evasive action to get away.

The results of Exercise 'Skyshield' were, perhaps, no fair indication of how the Vulcan would have fared in a real war situation, for in the European context it was unlikely that the V-Force would have had the benefit of a jamming screen thrown out by preceding USAF bombers to assist their progress; and, after the ICBMs and IRBMs, it was Bomber Command that would have been in the vanguard of a retaliatory nuclear strike.[59]

12 V-FORCE SUPPORT:
RECONNAISSANCE AND COUNTERMEASURES

In 1951, with the V-bomber production programme given super-priority status, the Air Staff realised that little current intelligence on the Soviet air defence system was available, and in July that year, in response to the growing need to gather electronic intelligence, No 192 Squadron was re-formed at RAF Watton, Norfolk, and armed initially with Lincoln B2 aircraft converted for the Electronic Intelligence (ELINT) role. The Lincoln was not really suited to the task; although it had a substantial range, it was slow and lacked altitude performance. In April 1952, therefore, No 192 Squadron was allocated four Boeing RB-29A Washingtons; these aircraft were part of the package of 87 B-29s supplied to the RAF under the Mutual Defense Assistance Program to fill the gap until the Canberra light bomber became operational.

Bomber Command returned most of its surviving Washingtons — about a dozen having been scrapped or lost in accidents — to the United States in 1953-4, but No 192 Squadron's aircraft remained in service in the ELINT role until 1958. In addition to monitoring land-based Soviet radar and signals traffic during sorties flown mainly over the Baltic and the Black Sea, with occasional runs along Iran's border with the USSR and trips to Bodo in Norway to operate off North Russia, the squadron also logged naval communications from Soviet warships. None of the four RB-29As was lost, although many interceptions by Russians fighters were recorded, particularly over the sensitive area of the Black Sea.

No 192 Squadron's missions were often dangerous; there were no guarantees that the Washingtons would not be attacked by Soviet fighter pilots. But during the early years of the 1950s a small group of RAF pilots, operating in conditions of the utmost secrecy, carried out a number of sorties that were perilous in the extreme, involving flights deep into the western Soviet Union.

In July 1951 Sqn Ldr John Crampton, then commanding No 97 (Lincoln) Squadron at RAF Hemswell, was summoned to HQ Bomber Command at RAF High Wycombe to be told by the AOC-in-C, Air Chief Marshal Sir Hugh P. Lloyd, that he was to assume command of a Special Duty Flight whose operations would be conducted in conditions of utmost secrecy. The Flight would be equipped with the North American RB-45C, the reconnaissance version of America's first operational multijet bomber, and the aircrew involved — nine in all, including Crampton — were to assemble at RAF Sculthorpe in Norfolk, one of the UK bases used by SAC, before proceeding to the USA for a 60-day period of training.

On 3 August 1951 the RAF personnel flew to Barksdale AFB, Louisiana, and spent 10 days familiarising themselves with the B-45 bomber before flying to Lockbourne AFB, Ohio, to become acquainted with the RB-45C variant. Lockbourne was the home base of the three RB-45C squadrons of the 91st Strategic Reconnaissance Wing; two were absent on overseas deployments and the RAF crews converted with the 323rd SRS.

One of the RAF pilots was returned to the UK after writing off an aircraft in a heavy night landing, luckily with no damage to his crew, and his place was taken by another RAF pilot already on secondment to a B-45 squadron. After successfully completing their conversion course, the crews returned to Sculthorpe and were attached to the RB-45C unit already in residence there. Neither the British nor their American hosts had any inkling about what was in the offing, and it was not until early 1952 that Sqn Ldr Crampton and his navigator, Flt Lt Rex Sanders, were summoned to Bomber Command HQ to be told about their mission, which was to carry out night radar photography of routes over which RAF and USAF bombers would fly to targets in the Baltic States, the Moscow area and central southern Russia. One of the principal concerns was to detect surface-to-air missile (SAM) sites (the Soviets were known to be developing a SAM system, although in fact this, based on the SA-1 'Guild', would not be operational until at least 1954) and to try to establish evidence of the deployment of surface-to-surface missiles.

Four RB-45Cs (three operational aircraft and one spare) were allocated to the Special Duty Flight; these were stripped of all USAF markings at RAF West Raynham and repainted in RAF insignia before returning to Sculthorpe. Before the first mission, Sqn Ldr Crampton and his crew made a 30-minute flight over the Soviet Zone of Germany while ground stations listened for unusual Soviet radio and radar activity that might indicate the flight was being tracked, but nothing untoward was noted and it was decided to proceed with the principal mission.

All three routes were to be flown simultaneously, the three aircraft departing Sculthorpe in rapid succession and heading for a point north of Denmark, where they were to make rendezvous with USAF KB-29 tankers. After taking on the maximum possible fuel load they were to climb at maximum continuous power at 0.68M until they reached the highest attainable altitude the prevailing conditions would permit. As they made their penetrations, the intelligence agencies would again be listening for signs of a Soviet reaction. Radio silence would be broken only in the direst emergency. When the crews were briefed they received three separate weather forecasts for each route: a genuine one and two bogus ones. One of the latter was to uphold their Sculthorpe 'cover story' and the other was for the benefit of Soviet interrogators if they were forced down and captured; the crews were to maintain that they had been involved in a weather reconnaissance of the Black Sea in the case of the southern route and of the Gulf of Bothnia in the case of the northern ones, and that they had strayed off course.

The first sortie was flown in April 1952, the aircraft taking off from Sculthorpe in the late afternoon. The three crews were: Sqn Ldr John Crampton, Flt Lt Rex Sanders and Sgt Lindsay; Flt Lt Gordon Cremer, Flt Sgt Bob Anstee and Sgt Don Greenslade; Flt Lt Bill Blair, Flt Lt John Hill and Flt Sgt Joe Acklam. The aircraft made rendezvous with their tankers and then headed into Soviet air space, all lights extinguished. Sqn Ldr Crampton's crew had the longest haul, southeast across the USSR, and he later recalled that his most enduring memory of the route was the apparent wilderness over which he was flying. There were no lights on the ground and no apparent sign of human habitation, a scene quite different from the rest of Europe.

All the target photographs were taken as planned, the navigators taking 35mm photographs of the radar displays, and all three aircraft returned to base safely, though not without incident; about twenty minutes before the first aircraft (Flt Lt Blair) was due to arrive at Sculthorpe low stratus started to roll in from the North Sea, so he had to divert to Manston. Sqn Ldr Crampton arrived during a temporary break in the weather and got in successfully, but Flt Lt Cremer, who had had to land at Copenhagen because of iced-up fuel filters, had to divert into Prestwick.

Unfortunately, when the films were examined it was found that the cameras had not been focused properly, and because of this the intelligence material gathered there during the first series of overflights was far less than had been hoped or anticipated. On 16 December 1952, after a thorough analysis of the early flights, Air Chief Marshall Sir Hugh P. Lloyd wrote to Maj-Gen John P. McConnell, commanding the British-based USAF 7th Air Division, and expressed his regrets that the operation had not provided the required answers.

A few days later the RB-45Cs, still bearing RAF markings, flew back to Lockbourne AFB and the crews returned to other duties, Sqn Ldr Crampton being given command of No 101 Squadron at Binbrook, the first to re-arm with Canberras. In October 1952 the Special Duty Flight was reactivated, with Crampton once again in command, but with some changes of personnel. His previous co-pilot, Sgt Lindsay, had been involved in a B-29 crash and his place was taken by Flt Lt McAlistair Furze, a flight commander on No 101 Squadron, known to all and sundry as 'McFurze'. The crews embarked on a period of intensive training, only to have the forthcoming operation cancelled early in December.

The Special Duty Flight was again activated in March 1954. Again the crews were briefed to cover three routes: north, central and southern; the latter was a long and potentially dangerous trip that would require refuelling inbound as well as outbound, and Sqn Ldr Crampton selected this one for himself. There was some comfort to be derived from the Intelligence briefing, at which he had been told that although his aircraft might be tracked by Soviet GCI, he was not likely to encounter radar-equipped night-fighters and he need not worry about flak, as he would be flying too high and too fast.

Late in April, the three RB-45Cs once again refuelled off northern Denmark and set off on their respective routes. Apart from the replacement of Sgt Lindsay by Flt Lt Furze, already mentioned, the only other crew change was in Crew 3, where Flt Lt Bill Blair was replaced by Flt Lt Harry Currell.

Having photographed most of his assigned targets, Sqn Ldr Crampton turned towards Kiev on the last leg. As he flew on at 36,000ft (10,980m) and a steady 0.7M he noticed what looked like lightning flashes twinkling on the ground far below. Then, as he approached Kiev, the sky ahead erupted with what he later described as a 'veritable flare path of exploding golden anti-aircraft fire', at the same height as the RB-45C and a few hundred yards in front. His reaction was instinctive; he pushed the throttles wide open and turned west, heading for Germany, a good 1,000 miles (1,600km) away. His destination was Fürstenfeldbruck, the planned air refuelling rendezvous and emergency alternative airfield.

Contact was made with the KB-29 tanker as scheduled, but because of a refuelling malfunction Crampton decided to land at Fürstenfeldbruck and top up there before returning to Sculthorpe, where the other two aircraft had already landed. Their flights had been without incident, and the results obtained on this mission were completely successful.[60]

On 1 June, 1955, RAF Bomber Command's strategic reconnaissance capability was transformed almost overnight with the re-formation of No 543 Squadron at RAF Gaydon, Warwickshire. In November it began moving to RAF Wyton under the command of Wg Cdr R. E. Havercroft, and by April 1956 it had an establishment of 10 Vickers Valiant B(PR)1 aircraft. In the day role, the PR Valiant carried up to eight main F96 fan cameras with 48in lenses to provide horizon-to-horizon cover, and a tri-installation of three F49 wide-angle survey cameras, all — with the exception of two of the wide-angle cameras — mounted in a camera crate in the bomb bay. Behind this, in a fairing, was another F49 survey camera, with the two oblique cameras of the wide-angle installation mounted above it. In the night role, the B(PR)1 carried five or six cameras in the camera crate, together with five or six photo-cell units. Photo-flashes were housed in a flash crate at the rear of the bomb bay.

On 9 February 1956, at which time it had five Valiants on strength, No 543 Squadron made its first serious contribution to V-Force activity when it took part in a Bomber Command V-Force interception trial, providing two aircraft out of a total force of seven Valiants and eighteen Canberras. The purpose of the trial was to conduct a study of V-Force penetration and interception problems and to observe the degree of success that the fighters and radar defences had in dealing with the penetration. The Squadron ORB records that 'both of the aircraft provided completed the briefed route, according to plan'.

With its crews only just emerging from the operational conversion unit phase, No 543 Squadron was not yet qualified to take up its photographic task. Instead, it busied itself with continuation training; in March 1956 it carried out a Continental cross-country training exercise for the first time, and in May it flew six sorties in the Bomber Command Exercise 'Rejuvenate', the purpose of which was to give Fighter Command aircraft interception practice in the sector covering the northwest approaches to the UK. On 24 June Wg Cdr Havercroft took one of No 543's Valiants (WZ394) to Idris in Libya to take part in Exercise 'Thunderhead', designed to test NATO defences in the northeastern Mediterranean. Another No 543 Squadron Valiant spent the summer of 1956 carrying out trials with 'Yellow Aster', which was the code-name for the H2S Mk 9, a non-scanning radar system designed to make it possible to carry out all-weather reconnaissance operations.

The Valiants were not yet fully equipped for their specialised reconnaissance role, and during 1956 aircraft were sent to Vickers-Armstrong Ltd, Weybridge, and Marshall's Ltd of Cambridge for modification, but as the fully-modified aircraft were returned to the squadron a series of seven-hour cross-country flights was initiated for general research into flight planning, fuel loading and aircraft performance. From 9 October to 29 December 1956 two Valiants were detached to RCAF Namao, near Edmonton, Alberta, to assess the effect of winter conditions on airborne radar equipment. Further phases of this exercise, called Operation 'Snow Trip', followed early in 1957; all the flying was directly concerned with radar coverage of various targets obtained from different heights with both radial and Sidescan radar. In May 1957 No 543 Squadron conducted its first operational reconnaissance during Exercise 'Vigilant', two crews flying each night to carry out radar targeting raids. Four very successful sorties were completed, and in June two Valiants went to Malta to give a demonstration of their equipment and operating techniques to representatives of Allied Forces Mediterranean (AFMED). Prior to the presentation, the Valiants flew several special Sidescan sorties; details are not specified, but the sorties may have involved flights to the Black Sea area.

Two of No 543 Squadron's crews were now declared 'combat' classified. The crews concerned were those of Wg Cdr Havercroft and Sqn Ldr G. D. Cremer (who, it will be recalled, had taken part in the RAF RB-45C sorties over the USSR some years earlier). It was Sqn Ldr Cremer who commanded a detachment of two Valiants (WZ391 and WZ392) that went to RAAF Edinburgh Field, South Australia, in August 1957 to participate in Operation 'Antler', the series

of British nuclear tests at the Maralinga range. During the trials, the Valiants carried out photographic and radar reconnaissance before, during and after each test.

In 1964, three Valiants and four crews of No 543 Squadron were positioned at Salisbury Airport, Southern Rhodesia, for Operation 'Pontifex'. This involved an aerial survey of Northern and Southern Rhodesia and Bechuanaland. The operation was under the control of the Central Reconnaissance Establishment and was believed to be the largest task of this nature ever undertaken by the RAF, covering 400,000 square miles of territory. During the operation, Valiant WZ394 developed a crack in the rear wing spar and had to return to the UK for repair. It was a foretaste of troubles to come: when other Valiants were inspected more indications of metal fatigue were discovered, and the whole Valiant force was withdrawn from operational service in January 1965.

As far as No 543 Squadron was concerned, the consequences were more immediate. Inspections of its aircraft showed that only one was fit to fly a limited number of hours; six of the remaining seven were available for emergency use only, to be serviced and made ready for combat as required.

Plans had already been laid for the PR Valiants to be replaced by the Handley Page Victor B/SR Mk 2 in 1967, but the premature withdrawal of the Valiant meant that the Victor had to be phased into the reconnaissance role sooner than planned. Work was accelerated on the prototype PR Victor, XL165, and this was flown at Radlett on 23 February 1965, being delivered to the A&AEE at Boscombe Down for acceptance trials in March. The second SR2 conversion was XM718, which had been rebuilt following a crash landing at RAF Wittering; this aircraft also went to Boscombe Down and was eventually delivered to No 543 Squadron in January 1966. The squadron's first SR2 was XL230, which was delivered to Wyton on 19 May 1965. Two Victors were on strength by June, four by September, five by November and six by January 1966. The eleventh and last aircraft was delivered on 21 June 1966; unfortunately, just a few days later, while carrying out a low-level demonstration for the benefit of Press photographers on 29 June, SR2 XM716 broke up in mid-air and crashed at Warboys with the loss of its crew. It was being flown by Sqn Ldr J. A. Holland, who had captained the first of 543's crews to convert to the Victor.

In terms of operational effectiveness, the Victor had many advantages over the earlier Valiant. It had a better altitude and speed, and its range was 40% greater. For day photography, it carried a battery of F96 Mk 2 cameras; for night work, the F89 Mk 3; and for survey and mapping, the F49 Mk 4. Three bomb bay canisters could accommodate 108 eight-inch photo-flashes, each of several million candlepower. One Victor SR2 could photograph the whole Mediterranean in a single seven-hour sortie, bringing back 10,000ft (3,050m) of exposed film for processing either at Wyton or at the Joint Air Reconnaissance Intelligence Centre at nearby RAF Brampton;

infra-red false-colour film proved particularly effective, giving a more efficient penetration of camouflage than infra-red black and white. Five Victors could cover the whole of the Atlantic in less than seven hours.

Maritime Radar Reconnaissance, in fact, was one of No 543 Squadron's priority tasks, developed operationally during the Valiant days; in September 1965 the squadron flew three maritime co-operation exercises, and the task became increasingly important as the Soviets continued to develop and extend their new long-range ocean-going naval forces. It was a role that No 543 continued to exercise until its disbandment on 24 May 1974, the operational task having been taken over by the Vulcan B2 (MRR) aircraft of No 27 Squadron.

On 30 September 1957, while No 543 Squadron's Valiants were taking part in the atomic weapons trials in Australia, No 199 Squadron re-formed at RAF Honington with Valiants in the specialist electronic countermeasures role. During World War 2 the squadron had operated as a unit of No 100 Group in the bomber support role until disbandment in July 1945. It had re-formed in the same role as part of the Central Signals Establishment at Watton, flying Lincoln Mk 2/4As and

Mosquito NF36s, but on 17 April 1952 it was transferred from No 90 (Signals) Group to Bomber Command, becoming a squadron in No 1 Group. Its main flying task initially was to provide radio countermeasures training for Fighter and Anti-Aircraft Commands, 39 hours and 20 hours respectively being allocated to these two Commands per month; eighteen hours of the operational flying task were devoted to Bomber Command, and eleven to the Royal Navy. Early in 1954, when the Mosquitos were at last retired, the squadron's establishment was nine Lincolns and one Canberra B2.

After No 199 Squadron's re-formation at Honington, the Lincolns and the Canberra were assigned to No 1321 Flight at Hemswell. The flight remained operational in the ECM role from 1 October 1957 until 31 March 1958, by which time its strength had been reduced to two Lincoln B2s, the Canberra having been transferred to Honington.

The Valiant had not been designed to accommodate an ECM fit, and many modifications were necessary before the first aircraft was ready for service with No 199 Squadron. The operational ECM Valiants were equipped with APT-16A and ALT-7 jamming transmitters, Airborne Cigar and Carpet-4 jammers, APR9 and APR4 search receivers, and Window

dispensers. Compatibility trials were carried out by a 'special' Valiant, WP214, at the Bomber Command Development Unit, Finningley; the onboard equipment generated intense heat, and special cooling systems had to be devised and installed. The jamming transmitters were contained in nine separate cylindrical drums, each about 3ft (0.9m) high, 18in (46cm) in diameter and weighing 200lb (90kg). They covered the metric and centimetric wavebands and were intended to jam enemy ground radar and air-to-air radio and radar. The whole kit was cooled by a water/glycol system consisting of an elaborate network of pipes connected to a special air intake and heat exchanger. Other items of equipment in the modified Valiants included a passive warning receiver system to alert the crew when ground radar was locked on to their aircraft, an active tail warning receiver, a turbo-alternator to provide the AC power necessary to operate the jamming equipment, and five separate sets of aerials connected with the ECM apparatus, situated in the nose, tail, both wingtips and beneath the fuselage. The special Valiants carried two air electronics officers and one navigator.

Bomber Command envisaged that the rearming of No 199 Squadron with the Valiant would cover a minimum of nine months, the aircraft being progressively delivered as they were modified for the ECM role. The squadron's function was to introduce ECM techniques to the V-Force, and once this requirement had been achieved No 199 Squadron disbanded on 15 December 1958, its C Flight going to Finningley to form the nucleus of a re-formed No 18 Squadron, which — eventually armed with six Valiants — would now provide ECM support for the whole of the V-Force.

In retrospect, it is doubtful whether the squadron would have proved very effective under war conditions, for six

Above:
Victor SR2s of No 543 Squadron, RAF Wyton. *MoD (RAF)*

Right:
View of the tail area of a Vulcan B2, showing the tail-cone housing ECM equipment. The aircraft is carrying a Blue Steel training round. *MoD (RAF)*

Valiants could hardly have provided an effective ECM screen for the entire V-Force. In addition, the jamming equipment was subject to severe limitations in that it could cover only a very narrow frequency band at any one time, and even then the jamming transmissions were only at their best when the aircraft flew port side on to the stations that were being jammed.

The real solution to the problem was for the spearhead aircraft of the V-Force, the Mk 2 versions of the Vulcan and Victor, to carry their own ECM equipment; this had not been possible with the first-generation V-bombers because too much space was taken up by the bulky navigation/bombing system (NBS). The requirement for the installation of ECM in the V-bombers had already been defined in December 1956, in a paper prepared by the Operational Requirements Branch. The paper acknowledged that Soviet defences were becoming increasingly effective against subsonic bombers, predicting that:

'These defences will become extremely lethal to the V-Force in three or four years time unless methods of reducing their efficiency are devised and the aircraft appropriately fitted . . . Some increase in safety can be achieved if the aircraft are developed to give improved performance — in speed and height in order to stretch the interception procedures and in range to give the opportunity to employ evasive routeing where possible. There is, however, a limit to these improvements which is set by basic aircraft design parameters and therefore other expedients must be employed to keep down the loss rate. It is generally accepted that defensive armament is not profitable in present concepts where air-to-air and surface-to-air weapons will ultimately constitute the most serious threat to the bombers.'
[61]

The paper went on to describe the Soviet air defence radar that was in place at the time:

be fairly vulnerable to countermeasures despite the possibility of using a substantial high-power transmitter on the ground as a countermeasure step.

'Although it is realised that alternative frequencies ground radars can be used to supplement the Token and Kniferest stations, it would take a considerable time for even the Russians to provide comprehensive cover on new frequencies. In any case, it would be very difficult to cloak such intentions from our intercept service; the same considerations apply, but to a lesser degree, to a possible change from VHF to UHF fighter communications.' [62]

An analysis of the Soviet electronic defences resulted in the development of three types of jammer for use in the second-generation V-bombers. These were the ARI 18076 'Red Shrimp' centimetric jammer, the ARI 18074 'Green Palm' communications jammer, and the ARI 18075 'Blue Diver' metric jammer. In the case of the third of the V-bombers, the Victor, the necessary modifications to accommodate this equipment were relatively uncomplicated, as most of it could be fitted into the existing area of the rear fuselage. With the Vulcan it was a different story because it meant that the whole of the rear fuselage had to be redesigned to accommodate the new equipment, and Avro suddenly received the instruction to incorporate it when the Vulcan B2 development programme was well under way.

As well as the ECM equipment mentioned above, the new fit included a tail warning radar known as 'Red Steer', developed by the Telecommunications Research Establishment at Malvern from an AI13 set, which had been standard equipment in the Meteor NF11/NF14 night-fighter. USAF SAC's ECM kit was more sophisticated, but also a good deal more expensive, and what would fit into a B-52 certainly would not fit into a Vulcan or Victor. In any case, the RAF's argument was that the key to successful ECM was to prevent an enemy fighter from attaining visual contact with the bomber he was meant to destroy, which in turn meant blocking the VHF frequencies used to guide him to his target, and noise jamming was as good as, if not better than, many other more costly methods. The four Soviet VHF channels in use during the late 1950s were well monitored, and all could be jammed by the ARI 18074 'Green Palm', which — like the wartime 'Jostle' used by No 100 Group — emitted a high-pitched wail. The Soviet fighters of the late 1950s also carried a device, developed from the German Naxos-Z of 1944, which enabled them to home on to transmissions from blind bombing radars such as H2S, so the H2S Mk 9A carried by the Vulcan and Victor incorporated a modification known as 'Fishpool', which enabled the radar navigator to detect enemy fighters below and, to some extent, on either side of the aircraft.

To accommodate the new ECM gear, the Vulcan Mk 2 sprouted a new tail cone, increasing the overall length by 2ft 10in (0.85m), and a flat aerial plate was fitted between the two starboard jet pipes. The rear fuselage bulge first appeared on the second B2, XH534, which flew in 1959 and spent

Above:
Vulcan B2A XM646, with No 9 Squadron badge on the fin, taking off from Waddington. The B2A designation was applied to Vulcans with an ECM fairing on top of the fin. *MoD (RAF)*

'The principal ground radar in the Russian C and R (control and reporting) system is the Token centimetric (S band) equipment. It is a multi-beam, continuous height-finding radar operating on five or seven frequencies . . . It is backed up by a chain of metric stations, most of which are now of the Kniferest type operating on 65 to 75 mc/s with apparently the additional ability to operate on frequencies up to about 104 mc/s as an anti-jamming measure. The Russians seem clearly aware of the vulnerability of these radars to jamming.

'The Russian fighter control operates in the conventional VHF band between 100 and 156 mc/s. The aircraft equipment is a simple four-channel set which rather restricts the flexibility of control. This suggests that the control may seven years on trials work with the A&AEE before being delivered to No 230 OCU in December 1966.

By that time, the Mk 2 V-bombers were fully operational; the services of No 18 Squadron had not been required for some time and it had disbanded in 1963, re-forming later as a helicopter squadron. The whole of the V-Force had now gone over to low-level operations, and in this new role the Vulcans and Victors carried four types of ECM fit. As well as the ARI 18074, 18075 and 18076 jammers, the ARI 5919 'Red Steer' active tail warning receiver (later replaced by the ARI 5952) and the ARI 18105 'Blue Saga' passive warning receiver (to warn when a ground radar was locked on), they also carried the 18205 L-band radar jammer, the 18146 X-band jammer (in the Victors) and the 18051, a system for dispensing rapid blooming Window and/or infra-red decoy flares developed by Microcell Ltd.

Fortunately, Bomber Command was never called upon to put its ECM equipment to the test in a real war situation, but the many exercises in which the V-bombers participated proved beyond all doubt that many of them would have got through to their targets in what would have swiftly become the nuclear ruin of the Northern Hemisphere. And it is a sobering thought that the Air Staff always anticipated that the V-Force, rapidly degrading through combat losses and the destruction of its airfields, would never be able to launch more than three sorties.

There is an intriguing postscript to the V-Force's reconnaissance and ELINT operations. In 1958 the Royal Air Force became involved in the CIA's U-2 reconnaissance programme, a move that resulted from the adoption of a joint targeting policy by SAC and RAF Bomber Command. At this time, in late 1957 and early 1958, the CIA overflights were concentrating in the Soviet long-range missile test centres (Tyuratam, Kapustin Yar and Plesetsk) and the nuclear test sites in western Kazakhstan. The RAF's forthcoming U-2 mission would therefore be to photograph the strategic bomber bases. These included Chernyakhovsk, Tartu and Sol'tsy, south of the Baltic; Murmansk Northeast and Olenegorsk, on the Kola peninsula; Lvov, Bobruisk, Bykhov and Zhitomir, north of Kiev; Voronezh and Engels, in west-central Russia; and Saki, Adler and Oktyabr'skoya near the Black Sea, the latter being one of the penetration areas for V-bombers operating from Mediterranean bases.

The first batch of four RAF pilots assigned to the U-2 programme (Sqn Ldr Christopher Walker, and Flt Lts Michael Bradley, David Dowling and John MacArthur) were sent to Laughlin AFB, Texas, to undergo training in May 1958. Laughlin was a SAC Base; SAC had taken delivery of its first U-2 (56-6696) there on 11 June 1957, the aircraft being assigned to the 4028th SRS of the 4080th SRW.

The RAF pilots went through the same stringent CIA indoctrination procedure as their American counterparts before beginning flight training. On 8 July 1958, Sqn Ldr Walker was killed when his U-2 broke up at high altitude, probably after going out of control, and crashed near Wayside, Texas; his place was taken by Flt Lt Robert Robinson, fresh from the British H-bomb trials at Christmas Island.

Speaking of British participation in the U-2 programme, at a joint RAF/USAF historical seminar held in the USA in September 1993 (at which this author was also one of the speakers), Air Chief Marshal Sir Denis Smallwood, whose varied appointments included Commander-in-Chief UK air Forces in 1975-6, commented that:

'It was held to be a matter of the highest security and very few people, certainly on the UK side, knew about it. We had four pilots for many years — they rotated, of course — based at Edwards AFB. From time to time, if I remember correctly, the U-2s would move forward into western Europe, particularly into Cyprus, and they would operate from there. The purpose of this bilateral agreement was that if the chips seemed to be down and one really needed to have a very wide-ranging reconnaissance programme using the U-2s, then the RAF pilots would be used . . . The programme on the RAF side was run by the Assistant Chief of Air Staff (Operations) in the Ministry of Defence. It was a subject that came up occasionally during the Vice Chief to Vice Chief talks. It was certainly a subject talked about between the respective chiefs at that level and, of course, the Central Intelligence Agency and the Joint Intelligence Committee in London were involved. In London, it was certainly known to the Defence Committee at Cabinet level.'[63]

Some sources maintain that the RAF pilots were responsible for 'between two and four' of the 24 overflights that were made over the Soviet Union. Whatever the truth, it remains classified as this book is being written in the spring of 1998. Only when the file is opened will the public history of the V-Force be complete.

13 V-FORCE OPERATIONS 1963-1968

Vulcan B2 XM603 pictured during a
detachment to the USA.
Author's Collection

With the issue of the first Mk 2 versions of the Vulcan and Victor to the squadrons of Bomber Command in 1960-1, there was no reason to doubt the assumption that the V-Force would remain a viable proposition for several years to come. The force had a considerable array of British and American nuclear weapons at its disposal; the Blue Steel stand-off bomb would shortly be in service; and negotiations were under way to provide the Medium Bomber Force with even more formidable stand-off weaponry.

At this time, the B-52 squadrons of the US SAC were armed with the North American GAM-77 Hound Dog air-launched missile. This 43ft (13m) weapon had small canard foreplanes, a rear-mounted delta wing fitted with ailerons, a small fin and rudder, a very slim fuselage and a 7,500lb st Pratt & Whitney J52-6 turbojet in an underslung rear pod. The missile was designed to carry a one-megaton warhead over a range of between 500 and 700nm (926 and 1,297km), depending on

the mission profile, and could operate between tree-top level and 55,000ft (16,775m) at speeds of up to 2.1M. The weapon was fitted with a North American Autonetics Division inertial system, which was linked to the aircraft's navigation systems and continually updated by a Kollsman astro-tracker in the launch pylon.

The first powered test vehicle was launched from a converted B-52D over the Gulf Test Range on 23 April 1959, and on 23 December that year the first missile was handed over to the 4135th Strategic Wing at Eglin AFB, Florida. This unit, armed with B-52Gs — the Stratofortress variant designed to carry two Hound Dogs slung under its wings — was responsible for supporting Category III Hound Dog trials in co-ordination with Air Research and Development Command's Air Proving Ground Center, leading to SAC acceptance of the weapon system. The first SAC Hound Dog launch was made by a B-52G of the 4135th SW on 29 February 1960.

All B-52Gs and, later, B-52Hs armed with the Hound Dog carried one pylon-mounted round under each wing. The Hound Dogs turbojets were lit up during take-off, effectively making the B-52 a ten-engined aircraft, and were subsequently shut down, the missile's tanks being topped up from the parent aircraft. After launch, the missile could follow a high or low flight profile, with dog legs and diversions as necessary. Later, anti-radar and terrain contour matching (TERCOM) modifications were introduced. At the missile's peak in 1962 there were 592 Hound Dogs on SAC's inventory.[64]

Although the Hound Dog — which was eventually issued to 29 B-52 wings — proved to be a very successful weapon

Top Left:
Public Relations was a constant feature of V-Force life. Here, a flight lieutenant shows a group of schoolgirls around a Blue Steel Vulcan of No 617 Squadron.
MoD (RAF)

Left:
Vulcan B2s of the Waddington Wing on their ORP. *MoD (RAF)*

Right:
Blue Steel Victors of the Wittering Wing on QRA. *MoD (RAF)*

system, it was never intended to be anything other than an interim air-launched strategic missile. Even before it was tested, the USAF had initiated a design competition for a true air-launched IRBM: in other words, a system whereby the launch aircraft would carry the weapon to its release point, after which it would behave like a ground-launched IRBM and follow a spatial trajectory before its warhead impacted on the target, over 1,000 miles away. Fifteen American companies entered the running to develop such a system, and it was the Douglas Aircraft Corporation which, on 26 May 1959, was awarded a design study contract and named as prime contractor for the new weapon system, which carried the original designation WS-138A. In February 1960 Douglas received a further contract which called for the building of several research and development test vehicles; the missile was now designated XGAM-87A, and the name Skybolt was given to it. Other companies involved in the project were Aerojet-General, which was made responsible for the missile's hypersonic (9.0M) two-stage solid-fuel propulsion system; General Electric, whose responsibility was the design of the RV carrying the warhead; and the Nortronics Division of the Northrop Aircraft Corporation, which was to design the weapon's stellar-monitored inertial guidance system, consisting of an astro-inertial system and a star-tracker linked to a ballistic missile computer.

The 38ft (11.5m) Skybolt, which had a range of 1,150nm (2,130km) — Douglas having decided to sacrifice range, weight and warhead size so that up to four individually-targeted missiles could be carried by the Boeing B-52H or Convair B-58B — was properly termed an airborne strategic delivery system. It was the first (and so far, the only) air-launched missile in the world in this class, and would have altered the whole concept of strategic air warfare. In 1959 the RAF also began to show a serious interest in acquiring Skybolt as an eventual replacement for the Avro Blue Steel stand-off bomb, in order to extend the life of the British airborne deterrent into the 1970s. Apart from that, RAF Bomber Command and SAC were then in the process of building up a very healthy working relationship, and the adoption of a single missile system compatible with both made a good deal of sense.

In March 1960, as the result of a meeting between Prime Minister Harold Macmillan and President Eisenhower at Camp David, a Memorandum of Agreement was reached under which Skybolt would be supplied to the RAF. The missile was still a long way off being tested, but it was envisaged that if all went well it would become operational with SAC about the end of 1963. It would now be carried only by the B-52H Stratofortress, the B-58B version of Convair's Hustler bomber having been cancelled in the meantime. The Anglo-American agreement was ratified in May 1960 by British Defence Minister Harold Watkinson and US Secretary of Defense Thomas Gates, and it was decided that Britain would buy an initial batch of 100 Skybolts, to be armed with British warheads.

On 12 January 1961, a B-52G made a six-hour aerodynamic proving flight carrying four dummy Skybolts. No problems were experienced, and in June the first production model B-52H began a series of aerodynamic flight compatibility tests. These were followed in the autumn by the first weapon release trials, when a B-52F (57-038) dropped a series of inert Skybolt rounds. Meanwhile, in March 1961, President John F. Kennedy had recommended the allocation of additional funds to the Skybolt programme, and this was approved by Congress.

By the spring of 1962 Anglo-American co-operation in the development of Skybolt was an established fact, with Avro Vulcan aircraft also taking part in the trials programme and a 200-strong British Joint Trials Force operating at Eglin AFB, Florida, from which all Skybolt trials were conducted. Then came a series of setbacks. The first live launch of a Skybolt missile, from a B-52F on 19 April 1962, was a disappointment; although the first stage booster worked perfectly well, the second stage failed to ignite. In a second live launch, on 29 June, it was the first stage booster which failed to ignite properly, and the missile had to be destroyed by the range safety officer. A third launch, on 13 September, seemed more promising; both stages fired successfully on this occasion, but then the missile suddenly veered off course and had to be destroyed. Both stages also fired on the fourth launch, which was made on 25 September, but the second stage burned for only fifteen seconds, with the result that, although Skybolt flew well, it fell a long way short of its planned range of 900nm (1,668km) on this particular trial.[65]

By this time, the whole Skybolt development programme had come under review by US Secretary of Defense Robert McNamara, who was having serious doubts about it. The original idea behind Skybolt was that it would form one point of a triangle of three US deterrent missile systems, the other two being the land-based Minuteman and the submarine-launched Polaris. McNamara's growing opinion, in view of the latest (and realistic, thanks to reconnaissance satellite coverage of the USSR) information on the numbers of operational ballistic missiles the Soviets had at their disposal, was that Polaris and Minuteman were sufficient to counter any foreseeable threat, and that therefore Skybolt was unnecessary. Moreover, the Skybolt programme had cost $500 million by the end of 1962, and all the USAF had to show for this escalating expenditure was failure. On 7 November 1962, McNamara recommended to President John F. Kennedy that Skybolt be cancelled. After urgent talks with Harold Macmillan, which resulted in the UK government accepting the sea-borne Polaris system as an alternative, President Kennedy confirmed on 21 December 1962 that Skybolt was to be cancelled.[66]

The irony was that while the Anglo-American talks were in progress, the B-52F trials aircraft took off from Eglin AFB and launched a Skybolt over the Eastern Test Range; the missile worked perfectly and reached its target, 1,000nm (1,853km) downrange in the Atlantic.

Above and Left:
A Boeing B-52H carrying four dummy
Skybolt air-launched IRBMs. The
missiles have different nosecone
configurations.
Philip Jarret Collection/Boeing

Top Right:
Victors of No 15 Squadron lined up
at RAF Tengah, Singapore, in 1963.
Via Jim Bowman

The demise of Skybolt meant that the responsibility for maintaining the UK deterrent would ultimately pass to the Royal Navy; in the meantime, the Royal Air Force's Blue Steel Vulcan and Victor squadrons would continue with QRA, while the free-fall nuclear attack squadrons became increasingly committed to NATO or, in the conventional role, to supporting Britain's allies and commitments overseas. Beginning in December 1963, detachments of the Medium Bomber Force were sent to RAF Tengah, Singapore, and to RAAF Butterworth, Malaysia, on a regular basis to act as a deterrent to Indonesia's increasingly hostile intentions towards the Malaysian State; the aircraft involved were mainly the Victor B1As of Nos 15, 55 and 57 Squadrons, but the Vulcan B2s of No 12 Squadron also participated briefly. In September 1964, as an insurance against possible Indonesian air strikes, the Victors of No 57 Squadron were retained at Tengah beyond the normal period of their detachment.

The presence of the medium bombers, with their capacity to lift a very large payload of conventional weapons, almost certainly dissuaded the Indonesian government from any

thought of using their Soviet Tu-16 bombers in an offensive role against Malaysia. The air defences were also strengthened in September 1964 by the arrival of eight Gloster Javelin all-weather fighters of No 64 Squadron from RAF Binbrook, while No 65 (SAM) Squadron, whose Bloodhound Mk 2 surface-to-air missiles had been undergoing tropical trials at RAF Seletar, was ordered to bring one of its missile sections to immediate operational readiness and prepare to defend Singapore. All these resources were put to the test in a full-scale air defence exercise which took place on 28 October. (Developed originally by the Bristol Aeroplane Co and Ferranti under the code-name 'Red Duster', Bloodhound SAMs were deployed in defence of V-Force bases in the UK, 1958-61.)

In 1964, following the growing sophistication of the Soviet air defence system, the whole of the V-Force went over to low-level operations, the Vulcans and Victors being equipped with an early form of terrain following radar. By this time the Valiant was no longer part of the Medium Bomber Force. Three of the original Valiant squadrons (Nos 7, 18 and 138)

Left:
Valiants being broken up for scrap after their withdrawal from service — an ignominious end for a fine aircraft. *Via John Hardy*

Below:
RAF Canberras based in Germany and Cyprus had a nuclear strike role and were armed with the 'Red Beard' bomb. Here, a Canberra B(I)8 rolls out of a nuclear bomb delivery manoeuvre. *British Aerospace*

Left:
Vulcans and a Victor at Goose Bay.
Author's Collection

Below:
Waddington Wing Vulcans deployed to Butterworth, Malaysia, in June 1968. *MoD (RAF)*

Right:
A pilot's-eye view as a Vulcan approaches Gan in the Indian Ocean on a round-the-world flight.
Via Roger Bagnall

had disbanded in 1962-3, two (Nos 90 and 214) had been assigned to the flight refuelling tanker role and three more (Nos 49, 148 and 207) to the Supreme Allied Commander, Europe (SACEUR) in the tactical bombing role, armed either with conventional or nuclear weapons. The latter were, initially, the US Mk 5/28 and the British-designed 'Red Beard'; these was later replaced by the Mk 43, designed for low-level delivery. All the Valiants were withdrawn from service in January 1965, following the discovery of metal fatigue cracks in the main wing spars of some aircraft.

At this time, the RAF Medium Bomber Force had at its disposal five squadrons armed with Blue Steel and nine armed with free-fall nuclear weapons, either 'Yellow Sun' Mk 2, 'Red Beard' or American 'Project E' weapons. Nos 9, 12 and 35 Squadrons were at RAF Coningsby with Vulcan B2s, Nos 44, 50 and 101 were at RAF Waddington with Vulcan B1As, and Nos 55 and 57 Squadrons had Victors, Nos 10 and 15 Squadrons having disbanded during 1964. In 1965 both the remaining Victor squadrons were converted to the tanker role, leaving the Vulcan to maintain the UK airborne deterrent during its remaining years. This it did until 1969, when the deterrent was handed over to the Polaris missile submarines of the Royal Navy. The phasing-out of Blue Steel began in 1968, when the two Victor B2 squadrons at RAF Wittering, Nos 100 and 139, were disbanded on 1 October and 31 December respectively. The missile continued in service with the Vulcan B2 squadrons of the Scampton Wing for some time longer; No 83 Squadron disbanded on 31 August 1969,

No 27 Squadron reverted to the free-fall role on 31 December 1969 and was later assigned to maritime radar reconnaissance, and No 617 Squadron also reverted to the free-fall role in December 1970. The primary nuclear weapon now used by the Vulcan squadrons was the WE177B high-yield retarded bomb, a modification of the weapon originally developed for the ill-fated TSR-2, cancelled in 1965.

By the time the V-Force relinquished its QRA role to the Royal Navy, RAF Bomber Command was history, having become part of RAF Strike Command on 30 April 1968. The cancellation of Skybolt had effectively denied the RAF a chance to provide a deterrent into the 1970s, and cancellations in other areas — the BAC TSR-2 strike aircraft being the leading example — had written finis to other projects to which Bomber Command had looked forward at the beginning of the 1960s. There would be no supersonic bomber to replace the Vulcan and Victor. Yet these aircraft had helped to hold the line in a dangerous and troubled world, and would have formed the first wave of the West's manned retaliatory strike force if war had come.

The V-Force QRA experience had been a unique one. In terms of striking power it was the culmination of RAF philosophy extending back as far as World War 1, but it was also the swansong of the British strategic bomber. It lifted the Royal Air Force into a new era, and then withered away. But the legacy it left — a legacy of pride, professionalism and expertise — was enormous.

Left:
The cancellation of the BAC TSR-2 in 1965 left no immediate follow-on aircraft to the V-bombers. Here, one of the TSR-2 prototypes (XR219) stands forlornly on the gunnery range at Foulness.
Press Association

Below and Top Right:
A Vulcan B2 of the Waddington Wing approaches and lands at Tengah, Singapore, on an Exercise 'Sunflower' deployment.
Author's Collection

Bottom Right:
Striking shot of Vulcan B2 XM595 of No 617 Squadron being readied for a night sortie from Scampton.
MoD (RAF)

Top Left:
A Vulcan B2 of the Scampton Wing, detached on a 'Sunspot' exercise, overshooting at RAF Luqa, Malta. *MoD (RAF)*

Bottom Left:
Vulcan B2 XL427, fitted with a Blue Steel training round, on detachment to Honolulu during a round-the-world flight *MoD (RAF)*

This page:
A Vulcan B2 of No 9 Squadron, NEAF Bomber Wing (Wg Cdr Ron Dick) approaching Ohakea with an escort of RNZAF Skyhawks during a goodwill visit to New Zealand. *AVM Ron Dick*

Left:
Chief Tech Piersey, the Vulcan's crew chief, appears somewhat bewildered on discovering that the RNZAF had appropriated 'his' aircraft with some neat paintwork during the night...
AVM Ron Dick

Below:
Still bearing its RNZAF insignia, Wg Cdr Dick's Vulcan lands at Singapore on the homeward journey to Cyprus.
AVM Ron Dick

14 CONVENTIONAL STRIKE FORCE

By the end of 1970, the whole of No 1 Group's Vulcan force had assumed the conventional bombing role as part of the integrated NATO structure. The force continued to exercise its low-level bombing role, in which the principal armament was now 1,000lb (534kg) retarded 'iron' bombs, and emphasis was placed on night operations to enhance survivability in a hostile environment. Vulcans were still detaching overseas, although perhaps not as frequently as they had done in the 1960s. One of the more striking overseas deployments in the early 1970s was made in January 1972 by four Vulcans of No 44 Squadron, together with 45 officers and 135 airmen from RAF Waddington. The practice deployment involved a

Above and overleaf:
Shadows of a giant: Vulcans cast their shadows on the surface during a low-level training exercise. *AVM Ron Dick*

round trip of more than 30,000 miles, and was the first major demonstration of British air power by the Medium Bomber Force in the Far East for some time.

The Vulcans, led by Wg Cdr Maurice Fenner, left Waddington on Sunday 23 January 1972, flying via Lajes in the Azores to Bermuda. From there they staged through the USAF bases at Omaha, Sacramento, Honolulu, Wake Island and Guam before reaching their first main destination at Tengah, Singapore, on 28 January, having lost a day by crossing the

International Date Line. As usual, following a now well-established procedure, the engineering and other support parties began flying out in Air Support Command VC-10s and Britannias three days before the departure of the Vulcans. They included six Transit Servicing Parties, each with an officer and eight men, who were positioned at the overseas bases through which the Vulcans passed on their outbound flight. Essential spares were flown out in Hercules transport aircraft.

From Tengah, the squadron carried out low-level training sorties around Malaysia, including some practice live bombing on Song-Song range near Penang Island. During these operations, the Vulcans were 'opposed' by Malaysia-based Mirage III fighters of the RAAF, which carried out numerous interceptions. One Vulcan flew to Kai Tak, Hong Kong, during the eight-day deployment.

On 4 February the Vulcans left Singapore for RAAF Darwin, preceded by their main support party. For the next 18 days they flew a rigorous training programme of hi-lo-hi profile sorties in northern Australia and carried out further conventional weapons training in the form of live bombing attacks on Darwin's Quail Island range. Facilities at Darwin were shared with the Mirage crews of No 76 Squadron RAAF, detached from their base at Williamstown, Newcastle, New South Wales, and one of the high spots of this phase of the detachment was a large-scale air defence exercise in which

Mirage aircraft worked in conjunction with other RAAF elements to track and intercept an attacking force of Vulcans. During their stay in Australia, two Vulcan crews carried out weekend 'Lone Ranger' flights to Williamstown and to RAAF Amberley, near Brisbane. At the close of the detachment, the Vulcans returned to Waddington via Singapore, Gan and Masirah, with a final call at Akrotiri. In total, they had been absent from the UK for five weeks. [67]

From 1977, Strike Command Vulcans and crews deployed to the United States to take part in 'Red Flag', the air warfare exercise held under very realistic conditions over the Arizona Desert. For this purpose the Vulcans deployed to Nellis AFB, from where they operated mostly at night and at low level, and despite the fact that the ground was not ideal for terrain-following some good results were achieved, demonstrating that the Vulcan still had the ability to penetrate advanced defence systems.

In the late 1960s, two of Strike Command's Vulcan B2 squadrons, Nos 9 and 35, deployed to Cyprus to form the Near East Air Force (NEAF) Bomber Wing. No 35 was the first to become established at RAF Akrotiri, on 15 January 1969, and was followed by No 9 Squadron on 26 February. The two squadrons gave a massive boost to the RAF's striking power in the Mediterranean. NEAF's responsibilities were both national and international; its principal tasks were to contribute to the force levels of NATO and to provide support

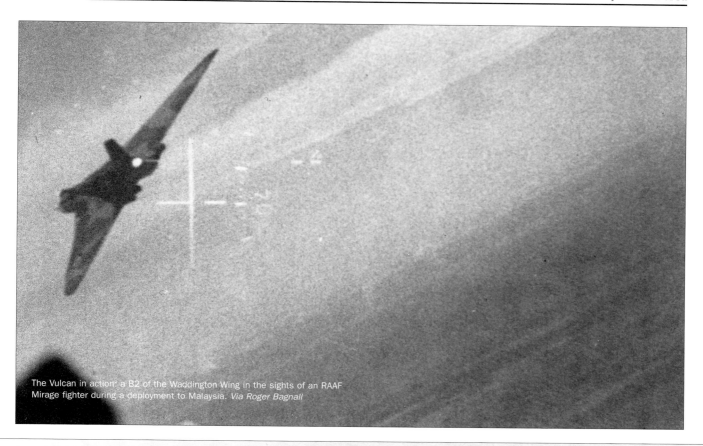

The Vulcan in action: a B2 of the Waddington Wing in the sights of an RAAF Mirage fighter during a deployment to Malaysia. *Via Roger Bagnall*

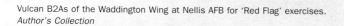

Vulcan B2As of the Waddington Wing at Nellis AFB for 'Red Flag' exercises. *Author's Collection*

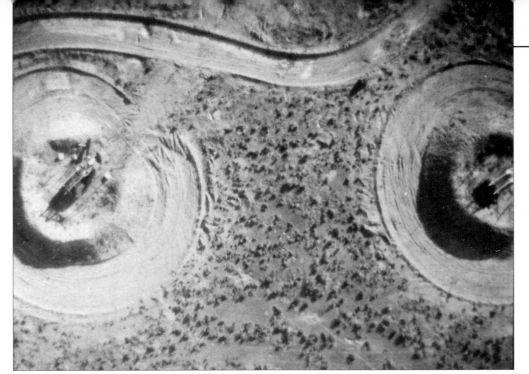

The 'opposition' which had to be overcome by attacking aircraft, including Vulcans, on realistic 'Red Flag' exercises: SAM sites and fighter airfields, populated in this case by time-expired RF-84Fs. *Author's Collection*

Right and Bottom Right:
Vulcan B2s of the Near East Air Force Bomber Wing (Nos 9 and 35 Squadrons), Akrotiri, Cyprus. *AVM Ron Dick*

for the Central Treaty Organisation (CENTO), whose member nations were the United Kingdom, Iran, Pakistan and Turkey, with the United States as an associate. The presence of a strong offensive element within NEAF became a matter of great importance when the RAF's last base on the mainland of Africa — El Adem, Libya — closed in March 1970, for it was correctly anticipated that Soviet influence in the area would greatly increase in the future.

No forces were actually allocated to CENTO, which had no international command structure on the lines developed within NATO; the function of the two Vulcan squadrons was to provide a tactical bombing spearhead for CENTO if such was required, but the aircraft would have remained firmly under RAF control. Because of the diversity of their task, the Vulcans carried out very varied training profiles, with aircraft detaching westwards to the United Kingdom and eastwards to Singapore, although the long-range sorties were usually undertaken by No 35 Squadron, with No 9 Squadron's operations restricted to the Middle East. The Bomber Wing was required to participate fully in QRAs and their associated 'generation games', the generation of nuclear or conventional weapons followed by a fly off. No-notice tactical evaluation exercises occurred at irregular intervals.

In the summer of 1974, the northern part of Cyprus was invaded by Turkish forces and the British Sovereign Base Areas were placed on full alert. The Bomber Wing dispersed, the majority of its aircraft going to Malta, and subsequently carried out a wide variety of operational tasks in support of the British forces in Cyprus. These involved, among other things, acting as airborne relay stations, cruising at 40,000ft (12,200m) over the Mediterranean and re-transmitting signals to points east and west. Vulcans had been called upon to carry out this kind of operation before, at various times; as

long ago as 1958, Bomber Command and RAE Farnborough had developed a system whereby speech from the aircraft could be transmitted to Bomber Command HQ at High Wycombe, or to other RAF communications centres, and fed into land-lines direct.[68]

The Turkish invasion precipitated the end of the NEAF Bomber Wing as such. As part of a political move, designed to help defuse an extremely tense situation in the eastern Mediterranean, the two Vulcan squadrons were withdrawn from Cyprus and relocated in the United Kingdom, No 9 Squadron going to Waddington and No 35 to Scampton. The V-Force was now entering the last years of its existence, but much still lay ahead of it in the way of achievement.

By 1979 the Vulcan's operational life had now been extended far beyond the planned date, and the progressive rundown of the V-Force began in 1980, some aircraft going for scrap, some for firefighting and crash rescue training, some as instructional airframes and others as museum pieces. As far as the units were concerned, No 230 OCU was the first to disband, in the summer of 1981, and this was followed on 22 December that year by No 617 Squadron. Happily, the squadron's absence from the RAF's Order of Battle was a temporary one; it was to re-form on the first day of May 1983 as Strike Command's second Tornado GR1 unit.

Scampton's other two Vulcan squadrons, Nos 27 and 35, both disbanded in March 1982, No 35 on the first of the month and No 27 on the last day. Like 617, No 27 later re-

Below:
Vulcan B2A XL390 of the Scampton Wing leads a Jaguar, Canberra and Buccaneer on a representative flypast to mark the 10th anniversary of RAF Strike Command. Only a few months later, in August 1978, XL390 crashed during display practice near Glenview Naval Air Station, California, killing its crew. *MoD (RAF)*

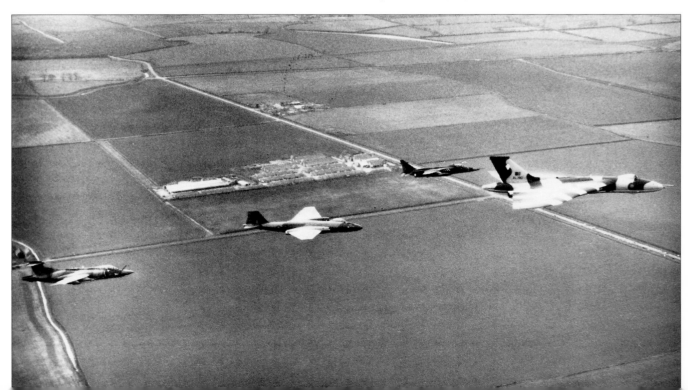

formed as a Tornado unit, but it was 617's old rival, No 9 Squadron, which had the honour of being the first to arm with the RAF's new and potent strike aircraft; disbanding as a Vulcan squadron on 1 May 1982, it re-formed on Tornados at RAF Honington exactly a month later.

Of the other three Vulcan squadrons, No 101 disbanded on 5 August 1982, to re-form as a VC-10 tanker squadron in the following year, and No 44 disbanded on the last day of 1982. That left No 50 Squadron, which continued to operate six Vulcans converted to the tanker role — a move made necessary by momentous events which, on the very eve of its expiry after a quarter of a century of first-line service, were to give the Vulcan its first and only taste of action, and assure it of an even firmer place in the RAF's hall of fame.

The British government's decision to launch a task force over 8,000 miles (12,870km) of Atlantic Ocean to recapture the Falkland Islands from Argentina in 1982 posed considerable problems for the UK forces earmarked to carry out the operation. Britain has a long history of fighting successful campaigns at great distances from home, but never before, in modern warfare, had her area of operations been so far removed from friendly land-based air power. Ascension Island, which was quickly to become the major staging post for 'Corporate', as the Falklands operation was known, was 4,000nm (7,000km) away, far outside the combat radius, even with flight refuelling, of any land-based British aircraft — except one — which might be capable of transporting a worthwhile war load to enemy targets on the Falklands. The exception was the Vulcan, still untested in combat 30 years after the prototype flew. When the Falklands crisis developed early in April 1982 the remnants of the Vulcan force were concentrated with Nos 44 and 50 Squadrons at RAF Waddington, the third and fourth Waddington squadrons, Nos 9 and 101, being on the point of disbanding.

No 44 Squadron was tasked with possible offensive operations against the Falklands, and the crews, drawn from the most experienced of all four Waddington squadrons, came to standby on Thursday 8 April, Easter leave having been cancelled. The 10 'fittest' Vulcans were selected from the aircraft pool, and on 9 April — Good Friday — Waddington's engineer officer, Sqn Ldr Chris Pye, was instructed to restore an air-to-air flight refuelling capability on these machines. This presented several problems, not the least of which was that the flight refuelling probes had been deleted from the Vulcan force some years earlier and the system blanked off at the probe connection. Some of the essential equipment, such as the nose-mounted non-return valves, was still in storage and fairly readily available, but locating the probes themselves was a far from easy task, and those that were available from stores were urgently needed for mounting on Hercules transports and Nimrod maritime patrol aircraft. Sqn Ldr Pye and his engineering team rose admirably to the occasion, and in record time a stockpile of probes was built up from time-expired Vulcans which had been allocated to museums or to various airfields for crash rescue training.

Ten Vulcans were quickly refitted with the probes, the fuel system tested to 50lb/sq in and ground fuel transfer exercises undertaken as a required step before the system could be declared operational. Intensive training of crews in flight refuelling techniques now began; it was 15 years since Vulcans had practised flight refuelling as a regular exercise, and none of the current crews had ever done it. Over a three-week period, the Vulcans exercised with the Victor K2s of the Marham Tanker Wing off northern Scotland; some bomb bay modifications were also carried out to enable the Vulcans to accommodate a full load of 21 1,000lb (453kg) 'iron' bombs instead of the low-level retarded bombs, which had a different release technique. A further modification involved the installation of a Delco Carousel Inertial Navigation System of the type fitted to British Airways Boeing 747s in five of the Vulcans to assist with long-range navigation over the South Atlantic; the systems were supplied by British Airways and were fitted in Vulcans XL391, XM597, XM598, XM607 and XM612. A sixth Vulcan, XM654, was also earmarked to receive the INS equipment, but in the event never took part in the forthcoming operations.

The flight refuelling trials were not without their crop of problems. In some cases it was found that Vulcans receiving fuel suffered spillage around the probe, causing a spray of fuel to float backwards over the nose and render the cockpit windows opaque. Several remedies were tried, including sealing the wiper hole on the cockpit lip, fitting a vortex generator in front of the windscreen and placing a colander around the base of the probe in an attempt to disperse spilt fuel. These refinements helped to reduce the problem, but a complete cure was never found. Yet another task for the Waddington Engineering Wing was to overhaul the Vulcans Rolls-Royce/Bristol Olympus Mk 103 engines and uprate them to 103% thrust for the operational task in hand.

On 23 April Waddington received a signal from Strike Command HQ asking the Engineering Wing to consider ways of fitting the AN/ALQ-101D Dash Ten electronic countermeasures pod to the Vulcan. The Dash Ten was well proven, having been used for some time by the RAF's Buccaneers, but some means had to be found of hanging it under the Vulcan's wing. This caused some head-scratching, until it was recalled that most B2s still in service had come off the production line with built-in hardpoints to carry the cancelled Skybolt missile. Even then the problem was not immediately solved, because no one could remember where the hardpoints actually were, and the relevant paperwork had long since gone by the board. So Sqn Ldr Pye's men resorted to trial and error, literally prodding at the underside of the Vulcan wing until they found two hard parts, disguised by two small and almost imperceptible fairings whose presence could not be accounted for. Further investigation revealed the long-forgotten hardpoints on every Vulcan except XM654, which had been one of the last few B2s to leave the production line in the days after Skybolt's cancellation, and which consequently had not been modified to carry the missile.

Above:
In the conventional bombing role, the Vulcan carried a formidable load of 21 1,000lb bombs. Two missions carrying this bomb load were flown to the Falkland Islands. *Author's Collection*

Right:
Vulcan XM597, the aircraft that diverted to Rio de Janeiro with a broken refuelling probe during the Falklands operations, landing at Greenham Common in 1983. *Author's Collection*

Sqn Ldr Pye's next pressing task was to devise some pylons, for none had ever been manufactured for the Vulcan, apart from those fitted to the Skybolt trials aircraft. Searching for suitable material, his team discovered some mild steel L-shaped girders on the Engineering Wing scrapheap.

Welded together, these formed the base of the pylon that was to carry the ECM pod. The pylons themselves were made in the local station workshops; these were simple, skeleton-like structures with a leading edge fairing, and the prototype was built and fitted to a Vulcan in three days. The necessary electrical cables were led through the wing via a series of tubes, never before used, which had originally been intended to feed coolant into the Skybolt missile, while the control panel for the Dash Ten was fitted into the AEO's station by the simple expedient of removing his cool air duct.

At the same time, it had been decided to fit a second locally-built pylon to the hardpoint on the Vulcan's port wing, partly for reasons of aerodynamic balance but also to carry the AS37 Martel anti-radar missile, which it was thought might be used to attack enemy radar targets on the Falklands from stand-off ranges. Modifications to the original pylon were carried out with assistance from British Aerospace, and as before, the wiring was led through the unused Skybolt coolant pipes. Two test flights were carried out by Vulcans with Martels on the port wing pylon, one to check aerodynamic characteristics and electrical compatibility, and the other to see how the weapon would function after prolonged flight at high altitude. On this occasion the missile was test fired after an hour's high-level carriage.

In the event, Martel was not used, as the USAF offered the RAF the use of a number of AGM-45A Shrike anti-radiation missiles. With a speed of 2.0M and a range of about 15nm (28km), the Shrike carried a 140lb (63kg) high explosive fragmentation warhead and was propelled by a solid-fuel rocket motor. Its operation depended on the carrier aircraft being illuminated by ground defence radars, warning of which would be given by the carrier's ESM/ECM receivers;

when within appropriate range, the Shrike's sensor heads would be switched on and the missile fired on target acquisition. After launch, the carrier's radar receiver continuously sensed the direction of the radar radiation emitted by the target and issued command signals to the missile's homing guidance system. It was originally intended to carry one Shrike missile on each of the Vulcan's underwing pylons, but it was subsequently decided to use the twin launcher of the type used by the US Navy's A-6 and A-7 aircraft. This enabled the Vulcan to carry four Shrikes at one time, two under each wing. Some delay was experienced in obtaining the twin launchers, which were not actually fitted and flight tested until the Vulcan force had been deployed to Ascension Island. Other configurations considered at this time included the possible use of Sidewinder AAMs on a twin launcher under the Vulcan's port wing (they were in fact fitted on the Nimrod) and the use of Paveway laser-guided bombs.

The first three Vulcans deployed to Ascension Island on 28 April, 14 days after their crews had begun air-air refuelling (AAR) training. During this time, each crew had undertaken three day and two night refuellings, the operations being supervised by an AAR instructor from the Marham Tanker Wing. These instructors accompanied the Vulcans to Ascension and on the subsequent missions, changing seats with the co-pilot (no mean feat in itself on the Vulcan's cramped flightdeck) for the link-ups with the tanker aircraft. For a week prior to the deployment to Ascension, the Vulcan crews also practised low- and medium-level bombing on ranges in the northern areas of the United Kingdom.

The Vulcan missions flown against Argentine installations on the Falklands were known by the code-name of 'Black Buck', and two aircraft were detailed for each, one as primary and one as reserve. 'Black Buck' 1, flown on the night of 30 April/1 May 1982, involved Vulcans XM598 (primary) and XM607 (reserve), although in the event XM598 developed a fault shortly after take-off and AXM607 assumed the primary role in the mission, which was a free-fall bombing attack from medium level with the twofold objective of rendering the airfield at Port Stanley unusable by Argentine jet fighter and strike aircraft and of creating as much disruption as possible among the enemy ground forces in the area. The crew of XM607 comprised Flt Lt Martin Withers (Captain), Fg Off Peter Taylor (Co-pilot), Flt Lt Bob Wright (Nav Radar), Flt Lt Gordon Graham (Nav Plotter), Flt Lt Hugh Prior (AEO) and Flt Lt Richard Russell (AARI). The aircraft carried a full load of 21 1,000lb (543kg) HE bombs fitted with Mk 497 fuses, some with 30-minute and 60-minute delays.

The Vulcan sortie was supported by 11 Victor tankers, flying in three waves. To conserve fuel, Victors and Vulcans cruised at 260kt (482km/h), the tankers flying at their economical cruising altitude of 27,000ft (8,235m) and the Vulcan at 33,000ft (10,065m), where its crew could maintain visual contact with the tanker force. This was some 7,000ft (2,135m) below the Vulcan's optimum cruise height in its heavily-laden condition and fuel consumption was heavy on the outward leg. The refuelling operation was a masterpiece of planning, with two of the Victor waves topping each other up and the third transferring fuel to the Vulcan, which descended to 27,000ft (8,235m) for that purpose. As each Victor completed its fuel transfer it broke off and returned to Ascension, until only the Vulcan and two Victors remained.

It was at this point that a serious snag developed. Victor K2 XL189 of No 57 Squadron (Sqn Ldr Bob Tuxford) was transferring fuel to its companion tanker, which was to have accompanied the Vulcan southwards to make the final transfer, when the aircraft ran into turbulence and contact between probe and drogue was broken. More turbulence was encountered as the Victors tried to re-establish contact, and XL189's drogue fractured the receiver's probe. With the latter inoperative the final part of the refuelling operation would have to be undertaken by XL189, so Sqn Ldr Tuxford switched places with the other Victor and reclaimed some fuel. The other aircraft, unable to receive, then broke off and recovered to Ascension.

Tuxford's next task was to find out if XL189's drogue had sustained any damage, so he signalled XM607 with a request for a visual inspection. The Vulcan descended and Flt Lt Withers tucked in close to the tanker while the crew tried to inspect the drogue with the aid of the AEO's torch, but they were unable to report by this means that the drogue was still operational. The only alternative was for XM607 to link up with the tanker; this was done successfully, and some fuel was transferred before the two aircraft broke contact.

The two crews continued the mission in the comforting knowledge that the final transfer could now be made. Tuxford, however, still had a problem in that he no longer had sufficient fuel reserves to fill the Vulcan's tanks before the final run to the Falklands, as he was supposed to do; XM607 had used more fuel than planned, and further unscheduled amounts had been used up when the two tankers changed places earlier. On the final link-up, therefore, the two aircraft were compelled to break contact before XM607's tanks were full. In fact, unknown to Martin Withers and his crew, Tuxford had given them some of his own precious reserves; when he turned away after the final contact and set course for Ascension, it was with the knowledge that unless he made rendezvous with another tanker, he would run out of fuel some 400nm (740km) short of his destination. To complicate the problem, he could not break radio silence to warn Ascension of his plight until he heard the code-word from the Vulcan signalling that the attack had been successfully completed. Luckily, Ascension had anticipated his need, and a reserve tanker was scrambled when the call finally came.

Contact was made without trouble and XL189 recovered safely to its base. Bob Tuxford's part in the operation earned him a well-deserved Air Force Cross.

Meanwhile, Flt Lt Withers and his crew had continued the flight at 31,000ft (9,455m) after the last contact with the Victor tanker, later coming down to 300ft (92m) over the Atlantic to avoid detection by Argentine radar on the mainland. Flt Lt Russell, the AARI, had now relinquished the co-pilot's seat to its rightful occupant, Flg Off Taylor, and the two pilots were able to concentrate fully on handling the big aircraft as it ran through strong turbulence at this low altitude. It was a relief when, at about 400nm (740km) from the target, they took the Vulcan up to 10,000ft (3,050m), its bombing altitude, for the final run.

This was made on a heading of 235° and XM607 crossed the Port Stanley runway right on track, thanks to the accuracy of the Carousel INS and the skill of the two navigators. The bomb run was straightforward using the NBS. The stick of 21 bombs was released to fall diagonally across the runway, the release occupying five seconds from first to last; one bomb exploded halfway down the runway's length and the remainder caused considerable damage among adjacent aircraft and stores. No opposition was encountered, although the AEO's equipment picked up a brief illumination by an Argentine SkyGuard radar. Flt Lt Prior used his Dash Ten and the transmission ceased.

Immediately after bomb release XM607 turned on its homeward course, climbing to cruise altitude to conserve fuel. With assistance from Tactical area navigation (TACAN), Direction finding (DF) and a Nimrod maritime patrol aircraft, rendezvous was made with a Victor tanker, and although a leak developed soon after contact was established, sufficient fuel was taken on board for XM607 to recover safely to Ascension Island. The Vulcan had been airborne for 15hr 45min. For his skill in successfully completing this, the longest-range bombing operation in history, Flt Lt Martin Withers was awarded the Distinguished Flying Cross.

'Black Buck' 2, the second Vulcan bombing attack on Port Stanley airfield, was also carried out by XM607 on the night of 3/4 May 1982, with a different crew: Sqn Ldr R. J. Reeve (Captain), Flt Lt D. T. Dibbens (Co-pilot), Flt Lt M. A. Cooper (Nav Radar), Flt Lt J. Vinales (Nav Plotter), Flt Lt B. J. Masefield (AEO) and Flt Lt P. A. Standing (AARI). Armament was once again 21 1,000lb bombs and on this occasion the Stanley runway was not hit, although there was substantial collateral damage. A third mission, 'Black Buck' 3, had to be cancelled because of adverse en-route weather, mainly strong headwinds.

The fourth mission, 'Black Buck' 4, took off from Ascension on schedule on the night of 28/29 May. The Vulcan involved this time was XM597, armed with four AGM-45A Shrike anti-

radar missiles, and its crew were: Sqn Ldr C. N. McDougall (Captain), Flg Off C. Lackman (Co-pilot). Flt Lt D. Castle (Nav Radar), Flt Lt B. Smith (Nav Plotter), Flt Lt R. Trevaskus (AEO) and Flt Lt B. Gardner (AARI). The mission had to be aborted when one of the Victor tankers went unserviceable before the penultimate transfer and was rescheduled for the night of 30/31 May as 'Black Buck' 5, with the same aircraft, crew and armament. Two extra fuel tanks were carried in the Vulcan's bomb bay, reducing the number of refuellings on the outward leg to four. The attack was co-ordinated with a Harrier strike on Port Stanley airfield, and while this was in progress the Vulcan stood off at a safe distance while the AEO attempted to locate and identify radar targets. Three missiles were launched, but it was impossible to assess results.

'Black Buck' 6 was flown on the night of 2/3 June, again with the same aircraft, crew and armament. XM597 made a low-level approach to the Falklands operational area, pulling up at a distance of 25nm (46km) to let itself be illuminated by the Argentinian Westinghouse AN/TPS main air defence radar. The latter was quickly switched off, and although two Shrikes were launched at other radar contacts, the radar transmissions were sporadic and not of sufficient duration for a full lock-on to be achieved. Nevertheless, one of the Shrikes scored a direct hit on a SkyGuard installation, destroying the radar and killing four Argentinian soldiers.

On the way home, the Vulcan's probe fractured during an air refuelling contact, forcing Sqn Ldr McDougall to divert to Rio de Janeiro, Brazil. One of the aircraft's remaining Shrikes was fired off, but the other suffered a hang-up and was still on its pylon when the aircraft landed. The missile and the aircraft were impounded and the crew, after being well entertained by the Brazilian authorities, were allowed to fly the Vulcan — minus the Shrike — back to Ascension at the end of a week. Sqn Ldr McDougall was later awarded the DFC.

There was one more Vulcan operation, 'Black Buck' 7, before hostilities ended in the Falklands. It was flown on 12 June by XM607, with Flt Lt Martin Withers and the crew who had carried out 'Black Buck' 1. This time, the Vulcan was armed with a mixture of 1,000lb HE and anti-personnel bombs, fused to burst in the air, and the target was enemy troop concentrations holding on around Port Stanley. The operation was held to be a partial success, and all the aircraft involved in 'Black Buck' 7 recovered safely to Ascension Island.[69]

So the Vulcan's career as a strategic bomber came to an end, in circumstances far different from those envisaged at the outset of its career. Fittingly, that career ended on a note of close co-operation between sister Services of long standing, the RAF and USAF; the same close liaison that had done much to assure the security of the West during the years of QRA.

15 V-FORCE SUPPORT
THE TANKER FORCES

The Americans, conscious that any offensive operations against the potential enemy — the Soviet Union — would involve flights over vast distances, were quick to appreciate the value of flight refuelling. The story of flight refuelling in SAC began in November 1947, when the USAF Air Materiel Command (AMC) asked the Boeing Company to provide a team to investigate air-to-air refuelling methods and installations. The result of their study recommended the full adoption of the 'looped hose' method, developed by the British firm Flight Refuelling Ltd, for all SAC B-29 and B-50 aircraft.

Just before Easter, 1947, Mr Latimer-Needham, then chief engineer with Flight Refuelling Ltd, received a telephone call from a US general in Washington, saying that he was arriving in the UK in two days' time to negotiate a contract for FR equipment, and to take back one complete set with him. Two B-29s duly landed at Ford in Hampshire, Flight Refuelling Ltd's base, and negotiations proceeded over the whole of Easter. By the time the US contingent left, complete with their set of equipment, a contract had been signed for the provision of a large number of looped hose sets, together with technical aid.

In March 1948, Boeing and Air Materiel Command conducted Operation 'Drip', which involved flight testing FR equipment in two B-29s. As a result of these trials, AMC asked Boeing to undertake an accelerated programme to incorporate the British looped hose system in SAC's B-29s and B-50s; at the same time, Boeing was also asked to begin development of a superior system. By May 1948, Boeing had converted a pair of B-29s to flight refuelling tankers, and had also introduced a new boom system design at the drawing board stage, which AMC authorised them to develop further. In addition, AMC now amended the design requirement to include single-seat jet fighters, which required a different method from the looped hose system. Late in 1948, while Boeing carried out the first flight tests of the 'flying boom' system, Flight Refuelling Ltd began work on a system for tanking fighter aircraft, and within four months had developed the probe and drogue method. The first dry contact was made in April 1949 between an Avro Lancastrian tanker and a Gloster Meteor fighter.

Below:
Vickers Valiant XD812 refuelling Lightning fighters of No 56 Squadron.
MoD (RAF)

Meanwhile, in February 1949, B-50A Lucky Lady II of the 43rd BG had made a nonstop round-the-world flight using the looped hose method. The first KB-29M tankers incorporating this system had been delivered late in 1948 to the 43rd and 509th Air Refuelling Squadrons at Davis-Monthan AFB and Roswell AFB, and it was the 43rd ARS that took part in this operation.

The first flying boom KB-29P tanker conversion flew in May 1949, and by the end of the following year SAC had activated twelve Medium Air Refuelling Squadrons, eight with an establishment of twenty KB-29s and four with twelve. Of these, four were fully equipped, five were partially equipped, and three as yet had no aircraft assigned. SAC's first KB-29P, 44-86427, was delivered to the 97th ARS at Biggs AFB, Texas, on 1 September 1950.

On 6 July 1951, a KB-29M tanker of Air Materiel Command, flown by a crew of the 43rd ARS, carried out the first air refuelling operation over enemy territory under combat conditions. Operating out of Yokota AB, Japan, and temporarily assigned to the 91st Strategic Reconnaissance Squadron, the KB-29M refuelled four RF-80 reconnaissance aircraft on a mission over North Korea. Meanwhile, one 91st ARS KB-29P, fitted with the boom system, had deployed from Barksdale AFB, Louisiana, to Yokota, where it was assigned to Detachment 2 of the 91st SRW, which was operating RB-45C aircraft. On 14 July, the KB-29P successfully refuelled one of the RB-45Cs on a combat mission over Korea.

About a year earlier, the decision had been taken to adapt the C-97 Stratofreighter to the flight refuelling tanker role under the designation KC-97E. Fitted with the boom system and laden with internal fuel, the KC-97E could fly fast enough to match the minimum speed of the B-47 Stratojet, and its entry into SAC service was to transform the B-47 into an intercontinental bomber almost overnight. The first KC-97E,

Above:
Two Valiants carrying out air refuelling practice. *MoD (RAF)*

51-183, was delivered to the 306th ARS at MacDill AFB, Florida, on 14 July 1951.

By the end of 1954 SAC had 32 Medium Air Refuelling squadrons at its disposal, 28 equipped with KC-97s and four with KB-29s. With the acquisition of additional B-47s and KC-97s SAC operations increased tremendously. About 142,000 air refuelling contacts were made during the year; operational training flights were conducted throughout the world, with more than 3,400 individual transatlantic and transpacific flights being made by individual aircraft. Up to this time, the majority of air refuelling squadrons were co-located with and assigned to bomber and fighter wings, but in 1955 SAC departed from this practice and organised two Air Refuelling Wings, the 4060th at Dow and the 4050th at

Westover, and assigned two KC-97 squadrons to each of them. The establishment of these two wings marked the beginning of a programme to concentrate SAC's air refuelling resources in the northeast of the United States. The build-up, which was to continue well into the 1960s, was designed to provide SAC with increased B-47 deployment mobility over the North Atlantic.

The last production line KC-97, KC-97G 53-3816, was delivered to the 98th ARS at Lincoln AFB, Nebraska, on 16 November 1956. Of SAC's 40 air refuelling squadrons, 36 were now equipped with KC-97s and four with KB-29s. The last of the venerable KB-29s was retired in the following year.

Early flight refuelling trials with the B-52 and the KC-97 had underlined the fact that the piston-engined tanker was by no means suited to refuelling fast, high-altitude jet bombers, which had to slow down and descend to a lower altitude to make a rendezvous. In August 1954, the USAF had announced its intention of buying an undisclosed number of jet tanker-transports developed from the Boeing Model 367-80 (Boeing 707) civil jet airliner, so providing SAC with an all-jet tanker force for future operations.

The first of these aircraft, designated KC-135A, left the assembly line at Boeing's Renton factory on 19 July 1956 and flew for the first time on 31 August. The first aircraft assigned to SAC, 55-3127, was handed over to the 93rd ARS at Castle AFB, California, on 28 June 1957. Some 400 KC-135As were eventually ordered for USAF service.

Despite Britain's pioneering work with the flight refuelling concept, the RAF was much slower than the USAF in appreciating the operational value of flight refuelling. Indeed, early in 1947 the Air Ministry decided that '. . . it was not a paying proposition,' and that it was 'not proposed to continue any further development of flight-refuelling equipment, but to rely on the aircraft carrying internal fuel for the ranges required'.

By 1954, however, this policy had changed; the Air Staff now decided that all Vulcans and Victors should be equipped for flight refuelling, and that it was desirable that the Valiant should be similarly equipped. This viewpoint was consolidated in 1957, when the Air Staff stated that it might be necessary to route some of Bomber Command's deep-penetration force (the Mk 2 Vulcans and Victors, whose planned combined strength was 120 aircraft) far around the flanks of the enemy defences to give them a greater chance of success.

HQ Bomber Command at first estimated that four squadrons would meet the tanker requirement, but later recommended that there should be two Valiant tanker squadrons plus a third 'shadow' squadron which would be formed at the Bomber Command Bombing School. The first flight refuelling trials with Valiants had already taken place at Boscombe Down in November 1955, using two specially modified aircraft, WZ376 and WZ390, but it was not until March 1958 that operational trials were begun by No 214 Squadron. This Marham-based unit subsequently became the

RAF's first tanker squadron, pioneering a whole range of single-point flight refuelling techniques, using the probe-and-drogue system developed by Flight Refuelling Ltd. The other Valiant tanker squadron was No 90, based at RAF Honington. Of the Valiants converted to the flight refuelling role, fourteen were B(PR)K1s and went to No 543 (Strategic Reconnaissance) Squadron; 45 more were B(K)1s, most of them equipped to act both as tankers and receivers. (The total Valiant production, excluding the two prototypes and the sole B2, was 109 aircraft.)

No 214 Squadron disbanded in February 1965 and No 90 in April, following the withdrawal of the Valiant from service. It had been planned that Victors would replace the Valiant in the tanker role, and conversion work had begun on a prototype Victor tanker in the spring of 1964. Conversion included the fitting of two fuel tanks in the bomb bay, a Flight Refuelling Mk 20B refuelling pod under each wing to supply high-speed tactical and fighter aircraft, and a Flight Refuelling Mk 17 hose-drum unit in the rear of the bomb bay to supply bombers and transport aircraft. The prototype tanker was XA918, the second production Victor B1, and after this aircraft had successfully completed its trials at Boscombe Down the Victors which had formerly belonged to Nos 10 and 15 Squadrons were converted at Radlett, the first conversion, XH620, flying on 28 April 1965. Work on the Victor tanker was speeded up following the decision to phase out the Valiants earlier than planned because of fatigue problems, and when

the first Victor tanker and four more Mk 1A two-point tankers were delivered to No 55 Squadron at Marham during May and June 1965, they were not full conversions, for they still retained their bombing capability and were fitted only with Mk 20B underwing pods. They were, in fact, rushed into service as quickly as possible to provide flight refuelling support for the Lightning interceptor squadrons, for the demise of the Valiant had left the RAF without air-to-air refuelling facilities.

No 55 Squadron, which had relinquished its bombing role in March 1965, was fully operational in the tanker role in June of that year, and during the weeks that followed, its Victor B(K)1As carried out a series of trials and refuelling exercises with the Lightnings of Nos 19 and 74 Squadrons, several involving trips to Malta and Cyprus. Meanwhile, work was proceeding at Radlett on the conversion of 10 Victor B1s as full three-point tankers; none of these retained a bombing capability and the first, XA937, flew on 2 November 1965 with the designation Victor K1. This aircraft subsequently went to Boscombe Down for radio trials, then like the others went to No 57 Squadron, which moved to Marham in December 1965 to convert to the tanker role. At a later date, three-point conversions were made from Victor B1As, the resulting tankers being designated K1As. No 214 Squadron reformed at Marham on 1 July 1966 with Victors K1/1A, while No 55 Squadron re-equipped with Victor K1A three-point tankers early in 1967. A Tanker Training Flight was also set up at Marham, flying a mixture of K1s and K1As.

Operations with the Victor K1 and K1A during the 1960s revealed a requirement for a K2 version, with a longer range,

increased power and greater fuel uplift, especially when operating from airfields at high altitudes in hot climates. Late in 1968, therefore, it was decided to convert either B2R (the designation carried by the Blue Steel Victor) XM175, which had sustained wing root damage and which was then in storage at Radlett, or XL614, which was in MU storage at St Athan, to K2 standard for trials. These were to be followed by 28 other conversions, which were to include No 543 Squadron's Victor SR2 fleet. In the event, however, the SR2s were not modified to tanker configuration, and the requirement for the K2 was reduced to 21 aircraft, some K1As being retained in service.

It was originally planned that the Victor K2s would enter service in 1973, but the conversion programme was subjected to serious delays by Handley Page's financial difficulties in 1969-70. Although Handley Page did all the design work for the conversions, the company never actually received a contract; on 8 August 1969 the Official Receiver was called in and the firm became a subsidiary of the K. R. Cravens Corporation of St Louis, finally closing down in February 1970. Later in the year, a government contract for K2 conversion work was passed to Hawker Siddeley Aviation, and the Victors — all surplus B2Rs — were transferred to Chadderton and Woodford, the former Avro factories where the Vulcan had been produced.

The first Victor K2 conversion to return to RAF service was XL233, which joined No 232 OCU on 7 May 1974. On 1 July the following year No 55 Squadron (Wg Cdr K. J. Lovett) became the first to equip with the more powerful aircraft. No 57 Squadron also re-equipped with Victor K2s from 7 June 1976. No 214 Squadron retained its K1As until disbandment on 28 January 1977, leaving Nos 55 and 57 as the RAF's only tanker squadrons. These, as we have already seen, performed splendidly in support of air operations against the Argentinian presence in the Falklands in 1982. The strong Victor K2 deployment to Ascension Island created a temporary gap in the UK air refuelling force which was partly filled by the conversion of six Vulcan B2s to the tanker role. Under the designation Vulcan K2, these were operated by No 50 Squadron until the latter's disbandment on 31 March 1984.

The Victor K2 continued in RAF service until 1991, operating in support of Coalition air forces during the Gulf War. The tanker role was then assumed by the VC-10s of No 101 Squadron, supported by the TriStar tanker-transports of No 216 Squadron.

Left:
The first Victor K2 arrives at RAF Marham, 7 May 1974. *MoD (RAF)*

Bottom Left:
Victor of No 57 Squadron refuelling Buccaneer strike aircraft of
No 12 Squadron. *MoD (RAF)*

Below:
Victor of No 55 Squadron refuelling Lightnings of No 11 Squadron.
MoD (RAF)

Left:
Phantom pilot's-eye view as he links up for a refuelling 'prod' with a Victor tanker. *MoD (RAF)*

Below:
And by and by, a cloud took all away... XM597, the display Vulcan, demonstrates its manoeuvrability one last time before retirement. *Author*

APPENDICES
1. THE V-FORCE SQUADRONS

Left:
A friendly rivalry existed between Nos 9 and 617 Squadrons, both of which claimed to have sunk the German battleship *Tirpitz* in 1944. A bulkhead from the ship became a prized trophy to be captured and recaptured by squadron personnel. Wg Cdr (later AVM) Ron Dick, OC 9 Squadron, is on the right, shaking hands with fellow conspirator Flt Lt Peter Armstrong. *AVM Ron Dick*

No 7 Squadron

Formerly an Avro Lincoln squadron which had disbanded early in 1956, No 7 re-formed as part of the Medium Bomber Force with Valiant B1s at Honington on 1 November that year. The squadron disbanded again on 1 October 1962, but later re-formed as a Canberra unit with a target facilities role. Disbanding again in December 1981, it subsequently re-formed as an air transport helicopter unit.

No 9 Squadron

This squadron re-formed with Vulcan B2s on 1 March 1962 at Coningsby, having disbanded as a Canberra squadron in July 1961. It later moved to Cottesmore and in February 1969 left this location for Akrotiri in Cyprus, where it formed the Near East Air Force Bomber Wing together with No 35 Squadron. It returned to the UK in February 1975 to become part of the Waddington Wing. It disbanded on 1 May 1982, re-forming as a Tornado GR1 squadron a month later.

No 10 Squadron

Re-formed on 1 May 1958, having previously operated Canberras, No 10 was the first squadron to arm with the Victor B1, and was based at RAF Cottesmore. It disbanded on 28 February 1964, re-forming on 1 July 1966 as a VC-10 squadron at RAF Brize Norton.

No 12 Squadron

Originally one of the three squadrons of the Coningsby Wing in No 1 Group, No 12 re-formed at that location on 1 July 1962 with Vulcan B2s. It moved to Cottesmore with Nos 9 and 35 Squadrons at the end of 1964, and disbanded on 31 December 1967. It later re-formed with Buccaneer S2Bs.

No 15 Squadron

The second Victor B1 squadron, No 15 formed alongside No 10 at Cottesmore on 1 September 1958 and remained part of No 3 Group until October 1964, when it disbanded. It re-formed on 1 October 1970 as a Buccaneer S2B unit.

No 18 Squadron

In July 1957, No 199 Squadron received its first Valiant aircraft at Honington, and its identity was changed to No 18 Squadron with a move to RAF Finningley on 16 December 1968. The squadron operated a mixture of Canberras and Valiant (six of the latter) in the ECM/bomber support role, disbanding on 31 March 1963. It re-formed in January the following year as a Wessex helicopter squadron in No 38 Group.

No 27 Squadron

The second squadron to arm with the Vulcan B2, No 27 re-formed as part of the Scampton Wing alongside No 83 on 1 April 1961, and in 1963 it became operational with the Blue Steel air-to-surface missile. The squadron disbanded on 29 March 1972, re-forming on 1 November 1973 in the maritime radar reconnaissance and air sampling roles with Vulcan B2(MRR) aircraft at RAF Scampton. Disbanding as a Vulcan squadron in March 1982, it later re-formed on Tornado GR1s.

No 35 Squadron

Re-formed on 1 December 1962, with Vulcan B2s, No 35 became the third squadron of the Coningsby Wing, alongside Nos 9 and 12. In January 1969 it left for Akrotiri, Cyprus, with No 9 to form the Near East Air Force Bomber Wing, returning to the UK in February 1975. It disbanded on 1 March 1982.

No 44 (Rhodesia) Squadron

Re-formed at RAF Waddington on 10 August 1960, No 44 initially received eight Vulcan B1s which had belonged to No 83 Squadron, the latter having rearmed with B2s. The B1s were progressively updated to B1A standard, the first — XA904 — returning to the squadron in January 1961. It rearmed with the Vulcan B2 in January 1968, disbanding in 1980.

No 49 Squadron

A former Lincoln bomber unit, No 49 Squadron re-formed with Valiants at Wittering in May 1956 and was later heavily involved in nuclear weapons trials, one of its Valiants (WZ366, Sqn Ldr E. J. G. Flavell) making the first air drop of a British nuclear weapon on 11 October 1956 and another (XD818, Wg Cdr K. G. Hubbard) dropping the first British H-bomb on 15 May 1957. During 1960-61 No 49 was one of three Valiant squadrons assigned to the Tactical Bomber Force under SACEUR; it disbanded on 1 May 1965, following the withdrawal of the Valiant from service.

No 50 Squadron

Re-formed at Waddington on 1 August 1961, No 50 Squadron received four Vulcan B1s and five B1As which had previously belonged to No 617. The squadron rearmed with the Vulcan B2 from January 1968. In 1982-84, having relinquished its bombing role, it operated six Vulcan K2 tankers, disbanding on 31 March 1984.

Below:
Vulcan B2 XH562 served originally with 230 OCU and subsequently with No 35 Squadron. *MoD (RAF)*

No 55 Squadron

One of No 3 Group's Victor squadrons, No 55 re-formed at Honington in October 1960 and was initially armed with Victor B1s, later receiving the B1A. In May 1965 it became the first unit to arm with the Victor B(K)1A two-point tanker and subsequently moved to Marham, where it received three-point tankers in January 1967. On 1 July 1975 the squadron became the first to arm with the more powerful Victor K2.

No 57 Squadron

Re-formed at Honington on 13 January 1959, this squadron

was armed with Victor B1s and later 1As and its career closely matched that of No 55. In January 1966 it moved to Marham where it rearmed with Victor K1/1A tankers, and on 7 June 1976 it received the first of its Victor K2s. Both Nos 55 and 57 Squadrons, while based at Honington, were deployed to Singapore during the Indonesian Confrontation of 1963.

No 83 Squadron

The RAF's first Vulcan squadron, No 83 re-formed at Waddington on 21 May 1957, receiving the first of its Vulcan B1s (XA905) on 11 July. Nine more aircraft were received by the end of September. No 83 later became the first squadron to become fully operational with the Vulcan B2 in December 1960, having moved to Scampton in October. In 1963, No 83 was the second Vulcan squadron to become operational with Blue Steel. The squadron disbanded in 1969.

No 90 Squadron

The second of the Honington Valiant squadrons, No 90 joined No 7 there in January 1957. From 1 October 1961 it became part of the tanker force at Marham with Valiant BK1s, and disbanded early in 1965.

No 100 Squadron

Re-formed on 1 May 1962, No 100 Squadron was the second of the two Victor squadrons at RAF Wittering, the other being No 139, and its B2s were later adapted to carry Blue Steel, the squadron becoming operational with this weapon in January 1964. The squadron disbanded on 27 September 1968, later re-forming with Canberras in the target facilities role.

No 101 Squadron

Re-formed at RAF Finningly on 15 October 1957, No 101 was the second front-line MBF unit to operate the Vulcan B1. In June 1961 the squadron moved to Waddington with five B1s and two B1As, rearming with the B2 in January 1968. It disbanded on 5 August 1982, re-forming as a VC-10 tanker unit a year later.

No 138 Squadron

The first squadron to receive the Vickers Valiant, No 138 received its first aircraft (WP206) in February 1955 at Gaydon, moving to Wittering with six aircraft the following July. In October 1956 the squadron deployed to Malta to take part in the Suez operations. It disbanded on 1 April 1962.

No 139 (Jamaica) Squadron

The first Victor B2 squadron, No 139 formed at Wittering on 1 February 1962 with an initial strength of six aircraft. In 1963 it rearmed with Victor B2Rs, equipped to carry Blue Steel. The squadron disbanded on 31 December 1968.

No 148 Squadron

Formed at Marham in July 1956, No 148 was one of the Valiant squadrons which took part in the Suez operation that autumn, one of its aircraft (XD815) becoming the first V-bomber to drop bombs in anger. In 1961 No 148 became one of the three Valiant Tactical Bomber Force squadrons assigned to NATO. It disbanded on 28 April 1965.

No 199 Squadron

One of the most experienced electronic countermeasures units in the Royal Air Force, No 199 Squadron had only a short career as part of the V-Force, receiving Valiants at Honington in July 1957 and changing its identity to No 18 Squadron with a move to RAF Finningley on 16 December 1958.

No 207 Squadron

Having previously operated Boeing Washingtons, No 207 Squadron re-formed at Marham in May 1956 with an establishment for eight Valiants, and in October had six aircraft in Malta for air operations against Egypt. In 1960 it was assigned to SACEUR as part of the TBF, and disbanded on 28 April 1965 following the withdrawal of the Valiant from service.

No 214 Squadron

Re-formed at Marham as a Valiant squadron in the Medium Bomber Force in March 1956, No 214 took part in the operations against Egypt later that year. In March 1958 the squadron undertook operational flight refuelling trials and subsequently became the RAF's first tanker squadron, pioneering many flight refuelling techniques. After a short disbandment (28 February 1965) following the withdrawal of the Valiants, No 214 re-formed once more on 1 July 1966 at Marham with Victor B(K)1s, continuing in the tanker role until its final disbandment on 28 January 1977.

No 543 Squadron

Forming at Gaydon on 1 June 1955 in the strategic reconnaissance role, No 543 Squadron was the second unit to receive Valiants (B[PR1]s). It subsequently moved to Wyton, where it remained throughout its career. Following the premature retirement of the Valiant in January 1965 the squadron changed to Victors, receiving its first SR2 on 18 May 1965 and its last on 21 June 1966. No 543 Squadron disbanded on 24 May 1974.

No 617 Squadron

Famous as the wartime 'Dam Busters', No 617 Squadron re-formed at Scampton on 1 May 1958 with Vulcan B1s, and in November 1960 received the first B1A conversion, XH505. From September 1961 the squadron rearmed with Vulcan B2s, and in February 1963 it was the first to reach fully operational status with the Blue Steel missile. On the withdrawal of Blue Steel No 617 reverted to the free-fall bombing role. It disbanded on 31 December 1981, re-forming as a Tornado GR1 strike squadron.

No 230 Operational Conversion Unit

Re-formed at Waddington in August 1956 as the Vulcan OCU, No 230 received its first Vulcans, XA895 and XA898, in January 1957, and by May that year it had seven Vulcan B1s on charge. In July 1960 it received its first Vulcan B2, XH558, and began to relinquish its B1/1As in 1964, so that by the end of 1965 the OCU was armed solely with the B2. It disbanded in 1981.

No 232 Operational Conversion Unit

Formed at Gaydon in June 1955, No 232 OCU's original task was to train Valiant crews and also to carry out intensive flying trials with the new V-bomber. The first OCU course went to form No 138 Squadron. On 28 November 1957 the OCU received its first Victor B1, XA931, and until 1964 was responsible for training all Valiant and Victor crews. With the demise of the Valiant it then became an all-Victor OCU, and in September 1961 it assumed the responsibility for Victor B2 trials at Cottesmore. The Tanker Training Flight at Marham was redesignated 232 OCU in February 1970, and continued to support the Victor tanker fleet until the aircraft ceased operations.

Below:
An Avro Lancaster overflies its direct descendants, the Vulcans of No 44 Squadron, on their ORP at RAF Waddington. *MoD (RAF)*

APPENDICES
2. THE SOVIET UNION: POTENTIAL TARGETS

Aircraft Factories	Co-ordinates
Arsenyev	44°10N 133°15E
Gorkiy	56°20N 44°00E
Irkutsk	52°16N 104°20E
Kazan	55°45N 49°08E
Kharkov	50°00N 36°15E
Kiev	50°26N 30°31E
Komsomolsk-na-Amure	50°35N 137°02E
Kuybyshev	53°12N 50°09E
Moscow	55°45N 37°35E
Novosibirsk	55°02N 82°55E
Rostov	47°11N 39°25E
Saratov	51°34N 46°02E
Smolensk	54°47N 32°03E
Taganrog	47°12N 38°56E
Tashkent	41°10N 58°50E
Tbilisi	41°42N 44°45E
Ulan-Ude	51°50N 107°37E
Ulyanovsk	54°20N 48°24E

Bomber Bases	Co-ordinates
Adler	46°26N 35°58E
Alekseyevka	49°14N 140°11E
Anadyr	64°44N 177°44E
Balaya	52°56N 103°34E
Bobruisk	53°08N 29°12E
Bykhov	53°31N 30°13E
Chernyakhovsk	54°36N 21°48E
Dolon	50°32N 79°11E
Engels	51°29N 46°12E
Lvov	49°49N 23°58E
Murmansk Northeast	69°00N 33°20E
Mys-Shmidta	68°53N 179°25E
Oktyabr'skoye	45°19N 34°07E
Olenegorsk	68°09N 33°29E
Ramenskoye	55°33N 38°10E
Saki	45°06N 33°37E
Sol'tsy	58°09N 30°20E
Tartu	58°25N 26°50E
Tiksi	71°40N 128°55E
Ukraina	51°10N 128°28E
Vladimirovka	48°19N 46°13E
Vorkuta	67°30N 63°55E
Voronezh Southwest	51°37N 39°08E
Zhitomir	50°10N 28°45E

ICBM Bases	Co-ordinates
Aleysk	52°28N 82°45E
Derazhnya	49°26N 27°16E
Dombarovskiy	50°46N 59°32E
Drovyanaya	51°53N 113°02E
Gadkaya	56°22N 92°26E
Imeni Gastello	51°09N 66°21E
Kapustin Yar	48°37N 46°18E
Kartaly	53°03N 60°40E
Kostroma	57°46N 40°55E
Kozelsk	54°02N 35°48E
Olevyannaya	50°56N 115°35E
Perm	58°00N 56°15E
Pervomaysk	48°03N 30°52E
Plesetsk	62°72N 40°28E
Svobodniy	51°24N 128°08E
Tatischchevo	51°42N 45°36E
Teykovo	56°52N 40°33E
Tyuratam	45°36N 63°24E
Uzhur	55°18N 89°50E
Verkhnyaya'Salda	58°02N 60°33E
Yedrovo	57°53N 33°42E
Yoshkar-Ola	56°40N 47°55E
Yurya	59°03N 49°17E
Zhangiz'Tobe	49°13N 81°12E

Note: IRBM and MRBM sites are not included in this list as many were mobile and easily dispersible.

Major Naval Bases	Co-ordinates
Archangel'sk	66°50N 50°13E
Baltiysk	54°39N 19°55E
Kaliningrad	54°43N 20°30E
Kronshtadt	60°00N 29°45E
Liepaja	56°31N 21°01E
Murmansk	68°58N 33°05E
Petropavlovsk	53°01N 158°39E
Polyarniy	69°14N 33°30E
Poti	42°09N 41°40E
Sevastopol	44°36N 33°32E
Severomorsk	69°05N 33°27E
Sovyetskaya'Gavan	49°01N 140°18E
Tallinn	59°25N 24°45E
Vladivostok	43°08N 131°54E
Zapadnaya'Litsa	69°25N 32°30E

NOTES

1. The Development of SAC 1946-1986; Office of the Historian, HQ SAC, Offutt AFB, Nebraska, September 1986, p2. (Referred to hereafter as SAC.).
2. Wynn, Humphrey; RAF Nuclear Deterrent Forces; HMSO, London 1994, p2. (Hereafter referred to as Wynn.)
3. Ibid, p8.
4. Ibid, p10.
5. COS (45) 285th Mtg. Confidential Annex, quoted in Wynn.
6. Quoted by: Gowing, Margaret, assisted by Arnold, Lorna; Independence and Deterrence: Britain and Atomic Energy 1939-1952, Vol I: Policy Making; Macmillan, London, 1974, p178.
7. Wynn, p30.
8. Jackson, Robert; V-Bombers; Ian Allan Ltd, Shepperton, 1981, p10.
9. Barnes, C. H.; Shorts Aircraft Since 1900; Putnam & Co, 1967, p428.
10. Jackson, Robert; Combat Aircraft Prototypes Since 1945: Airlife, Shrewsbury, 1985, pp12-14.
11. Jackson, Robert; Avro Vulcan; Patrick Stephens, Cambridge, 1984, pp18-22.
12. Jackson, Robert; V-Bombers; p13.
13. Jarrell, Howard R.; 'I was Forced Down in Russia', RAF Flying Review, June 1957.
14. Nemecek, Vaclav; The History of Soviet Aircraft from 1918; Willow Books, London, 1986, pp167-169.
15. Cochran, Thomas B., Arkin, William M., Norris, Robert S., Sands, Jeffrey I. (Eds); Soviet Nuclear Weapons, Nuclear Weapons Databook Vol IV; Harper & Row, 1989; prepared by the Natural Resources Defense Council, Inc, p6.
16. Ibid, p349.
17. Jackson, Robert; Combat Aircraft Prototypes; pp63-5.
18. Soviet Nuclear Weapons; p7.
19. Ibid, p349.
20. Ibid, p7, footnote.
21. Jackson, Robert; The Berlin Airlift; Patrick Stephens Ltd, 1988, pp 69-70.
22. Schroeder, MSgt C. (Ed MSgt V. L. Briley); A History of Third Air Force 1940-1988 ; 3rd AF Historical Pamphlet, 1988.
23. Wynn, p59.
24. Rowlands, AM Sir John; 'The Origins and Development

of the British Strategic Nuclear Deterrent Forces, 1945-1960', Proceedings No 7, Royal Air Force Historical Society, 23 October 1989.
25. Wynn, p95.
26. Wynn, p118.
27. No 138 Squadron ORB.
28. Jackson, V-Bombers, p24.
29. Norris, R.S.; Questions on the British H-Bomb ; Nuclear Weapons Databook working paper, National Resources Defense Council, Washington DC, 1992; Appendix 1.
30. Wynn, pp172-3.
31. Norris, Questions on the British H-Bomb; p1.
32. Jackson, Robert; Canberra; the Operational Record; Airlife, Shrewsbury, 1988, p70.
33. Norris, Questions on the British H-Bomb; p17.
34. Lee ACM, Sir David; Wings in the Sun: a History of the Royal Air Force in the Mediterranean 1945-1986; HMSO, London, 1989 and Jackson, Robert; Suez: The Forgotten Invasion; Airlife, Shrewsbury, 1996.
35. Wood, Flt Lt W. C.; 'The Vulcan — Second of the V-Bombers', Air Clues, Handling Squadron, Boscombe Down.
36. For a detailed account of this incident, see Jackson, Avro Vulcan; pp39-47.
37. 'Flying the Victor — the Third of Britain's V-Bombers', Air Clues, Handling Squadron, Boscombe Down, November 1958.
38. Jackson, V-Bombers; pp74-5.
39. Wynn, p148.
40. Ibid, p227.
41. Ibid, p229.
42. No 49 Squadron ORB.
43. Norris, Questions on the British H-Bomb; p21 and Wynn, p236.
44. Norris, Questions on the British H-Bomb; Appendix 1.
45. Wynn, pp242-251.
46. Jackson, Robert; Hawker Hunter: the Operational Record; Airlife, Shrewsbury, 1989, pp64-6.
47. Wynn, pp261-2.
48. SAC, p61.
49. Gunston, Bill; Illustrated Encyclopaedia of the World's Rockets and Missiles; Leisure Books, London, 1979, p60.
50. Ibid, p61.
51. Coulson, Sqn Ldr P. G., MBE; 'Lion's Roar', Air Clues; November 1959.

52. CAB131/13, D(53)5, 29 January 1953, PRO, London.

53. AIR 8/2201, COS(56)451, 14 December 1956, PRO, London.

54. Wynn, pp252-70.

55. Jackson, V-Bombers, p58.

56. Jackson, Robert, Combat Aircraft Prototypes; pp44-5.

57. For a full technical description of Blue Steel, see Francis, R. H., MSc, FRAeS; 'The Development of Blue Steel', Journal of the Royal Aeronautical Society, May 1964.

58. Jackson, V-Bombers; pp98-106.

59. Jackson, Avro Vulcan; p84.

60. Crampton, Sqn Ldr John; Bracknell Paper No 7, pp118-125 from Air Intelligence symposium jointly sponsored by the RAF Historical Society and the RAF Staff College, Bracknell, 1997.

61. Quoted in Wynn, pp181-185.

62. Ibid.

63. Smallwood, ACM Sir Denis; 'Seeing off the Bear', extract from a paper delivered at a symposium on Anglo-American air power co-operation during the Cold War; reproduced in the Proceedings; Ed Roger G. Miller, Washington DC, 1995.

64. Gunston, p136.

65. Jackson, Avro Vulcan; p108.

66. SAC, p110.

67. Jackson, Avro Vulcan; pp154-5.

68. Ibid, pp136-147.

69. Ibid, pp158-167.

Below:
A Phantom of No 56 Squadron hooked up to a Victor K2 of No 55 Squadron.
John Hardy

INDEX

Aircraft, types of:
Armstrong Whitworth AW52 17
Avro
Lancaster 14
Lancastrian 139
Lincoln 33, 105, 108
Type 698 Vulcan
B.Mk.1 . . . . .17, 19, 35,
. . . . .57-65, 72-5, 77-8, 87
B.Mk.1A 78, 82, 96
B.Mk.2 . . . . .80, 93, 95, 99,
. . . . .110, 111, 119, 123, 129-138
B2 (MRR) 108
Type 707 .1
BAC TSR-2 123
Boeing
B-29 . . . . . . .9-11, 14, 19, 22, 30-1, 33, 83,
. . . . .105-6, 139
KB-29 . . . . .105-6, 140-1
RB-29 .105
B-47 .140-1
B-50 . . . . .139, 140
B-52 . . . . .113-4, 117-8
KC-97 140-1
KC-135 141
British Aerospace VC-10 145
Convair
B-36 . . . . .24, 27
B-58 117
De Havilland
DH108 17
Hornet .83
Mosquito 83
Vampire 83
English Electric
Canberra 14, 30, 33, 37, 45-6, 52-6,
. . . . .68-70, 74, 84, 86, 95, 108
Lightning 20, 85-6
Gloster
Javelin 86, 19
Meteor 83-4, 111, 139
Handley Page
Hastings 33-4, 43, 46
HP80 Victor
B.Mk.1 . . . . .19, 35, 65-7, 74, 87
B.Mk.1A 96, 119
B.Mk.2 . . . . .95-6, 99, 110, 111, 123
B/SR 2 107-8
K.1/1A 144
K.2 . . . . .137-8, 144-5
Manx .17
Hawker Hunter 74-5, 84, 86
Horten Ho IX 17
Ilyushin Il-28 Beagle 55-6, 90
Lockheed F-104 Starfighter 86
TriStar .145
U-2 . . . . .89, 90, 112
Messerschmitt Me 163 17
MiG-15 . . . . .33, 55, 84

MiG-17 86
MiG-21 90
Myasishchev
Mya-4 Bison 27
DVB-202 24
North American
F-86 84
RB-45C 105-6
Northrop
XB-35 .17
YB-49 .17
Republic F-105 90
Short
Sperrin 35
Sunderland 33
Supermarine
Swift 84
Tupolev
Tu-4 Bull 22, 24, 27
Tu-16 (Tu-88) Badger 27, 119
Tu-64 .22
Tu-80 . . . . .23, 27
Tu-85 .27
Tu-95 Bear 95
Vickers
Type 660/667 Valiant
B. Mk.1 . . . . .19-21, 30, 33, 35, 37-41, 43,
. . .52-6, 68-74, 91, 93, 97, 109, 119, 123
B(K)1 .143
B(PR)1 106-7
B.Mk.2 38
Windsor 33
Air Bases (military):
Adler (USSR) 27, 112
Aldergrove 102
Alekseyevka (USSR) 28
Anadyr (USSR) 28
Bardney .91
Barksdale (USAF) 105
Belaya (USSR) 28
Belogersk (USSR) 28
Binbrook 119
Bobruisk (USSR) 27, 112
Boscombe Down (A&AEE) 60, 67, 96,
. . . . .102, 107
Brawdy .102
Breighton 91
Burtonwood 102
Butterworth (RAAF) 119
Bykhov (USSR) 27, 112
Caistor .91
Carnaby .91
Catfoss .91
Chernyakhovsk (USSR) 27, 112
Coleby Grange 91
Coningsby 123
Cottesmore 67
Cranwell 102
Darwin, RAAF 130

Debden .15
Dolon (USSR) 28
Driffield .91
Duxford .15
Edinburgh (RAAF) 44, 107
Eglin (USAF) 113, 117
Elvington 102
Engels (USSR) 27, 112
Farnborough (RAE) 15
Feltwell .89
Finningley 65, 109
Folkingham 91
Full Sutton 91
Gaydon 36-7, 106
Harrington 91
Hemswell 91, 105
Honington 43, 67, 93, 108
Kemble .102
Kinloss .102
Lakenheath 30, 89
Laughlin (USAF) 112
Leconfield 102
Leeming 102
Legnitsa (Pol) 27
Leuchars 102
Lindholme 37
Llanbedr (RAE) 102
Lockbourne (USAF) 105
Lossiemouth 102
Ludford Magna 91
Luqa 52
Lvov (Pol/USSR) 27, 112
Lyneham 102
Machrihanish 102
Manston 102
Maralinga (RAAF) 43-44, 70, 105
Marham 30, 43, 52, 93
Melton Mowbray 91
Mepal 91
Middleton St George 102
Murmansk NE (USSR) 112
Mys-Schmidta (USSR) 28
North Luffenham 91
North Pickenham 91
Oktyabrskoya (USSR) 27, 112
Olenegorsk (USSR) 27, 112
Pershore 102
Polebrook 91
St Mawgan 102
Saki (USSR) 112
Scampton 30-1, 65, 100, 123
Sculthorpe 89, 105-6
Seletar .119
Shawbury 102
Shepherds Grove 91
Soltsy (USSR) 27, 112
Spassk (USSR) 22
Tartu (USSR) 27, 112
Tavrichanka (USSR) 22

Tengah .119
Tuddenham 91
Tushino (USSR) 27
Valley 102
Vandenberg 89, 91
Vinnitsa .27
Vorkuta (USSR) 27
Voronezh (USSR) 27, 112
Waddington 30, 93, 95, 123, 129, 135
West Raynham 105
Wittering 33-5, 37-40, 43, 51, 99,
. . . . .100, 107, 123
Wyton 45, 106-7
Yeovilton 102
Zhitomir (USSR) 27, 112

Airfields, Civil:
Bedford (RAE) 102
Filton 102
'Foxwarren' 19, 21
London Airport 65
Prestwick 102
Radlett .107
Tarrant Rushton 102
Weybridge 19
Wisley 21
Woodford 57, 97

Acklam, Flt Sgt Joe 106
Aldermaston (AWRE) 15, 43
Anderson, Maj Rudolf 90
Anstee, Flt Sgt Bob 106
Atomic Energy Commission 28
Attlee, Clement 31, 45

Bailey, Sqn Ldr G M 70
Barnett, AM Denis 53
Bates, Flt Lt R N 70
Beeson, Flg Off R L 69
Bennett, E N K 65
Beria, Lavrenti 42, 43
Berlin Crisis (1948-9) 30, 33, 83
Blair, Flt Lt Bill 106
Bower, Wg Cdr D 65
Boxer, Wg Cdr A H C 43
Boyle, ACM Sir Dermot 93
Bradley, Flt Lt Michael 112
Broadhurst, ACM Sir Harry 65, 87
Brooking, Adml 33
Braun, Wernher von 87
Bruce-Smith, Flt Lt P 70
Bryce, G.R. 21
Burnett, Wng Cdr W J 43

Calder, Sqn Ldr C C 60
Campania, HMS 33
Castle, Flt Lt D 138
Chadwick, Roy 17
Cheshire, Gp Capt Leonard VC 15
Churchill, W S 45, 93
Cockcroft, Prof J D 27, 15
Cole, Sterling 45
Cook, Sir William 45
Cooper, Flt Lt M A 138
Crampton, Sqn Ldr John 105-6
Cremer, Flt Lt Gordon 106-7
Cross, AVM K B B 71, 74
Cuban Crisis 89-91, 104
Currell, Flt Lt Harry 106

Dibbens, Flt Lt D T 138
Dick, AVM Ron 88

Dickson, ACM Sir William 93
Dodd, Wng Cdr F L 63
Dowling, Flt Lt David 112
Dunne, Flt Lt T E 35

Eden, Anthony 53
Edwards, George R 19
Eisenhower, Dwight D 45, 87, 17
Electronic Equipment:
AN/ALQ-101D Dash Ten 135
ARI18074 112
ARI18075 112
ARI18076 112
Blue Diver 111
Blue Saga 112
Fishpool 111
Green Satin 43
Green Palm 111
H2S Mk 9A 111
Jostle 111
Indigo Violet 86
Naxos-Z 111
Red Shrimp 111
Red Steer 112
Token 111
TRE Type 80 85

Falk, Roly 57
Fenner, Wg Cdr Maurice 129
Finch, Gp Capt 58
Flavell, Sqn Ldr E J G 44
Flight Refuelling Ltd 139
Ford, Plt Off 44
Fort Halstead (AWRE) 15
Foster, Sqn Ldr Brian 21
Frank, Wg Cdr D A 65
Fursov Atomic Pile 23
Furze, Flt Lt R MacA 106

Gardner, Flt Lt B 138
Gates, Thomas 117
GEN 75 Committee 15, 17
Giddings, Wg Cdr K C 67
Graham, Flt Lt Gordon 137
Green, Wg Cdr D A 67
Greenslade, Sgt Don 106

Harwell (AWRE) 15
Havercroft, Wg Cdr R E 106-7
Hazelden, Sqn Ldr H G 65
High Explosive Research (HER) 33
Hill, Flt Lt John 106
Himmler, Heinrich 23
Hiroshima 9, 23
Hodges, Gp Capt Louis 53
Holland, Sqn Ldr J A 107
Hood, Flt Lt E J 69
Howard, Sqn Ldr Donald 65
Hubbard, Wg Cdr K G 43, 69
Hunting Engineering Ltd 15

Keightley, Gen Sir Charles 53
Kennedy, John F 90, 117
Kenney, Gen George C 10
Khrushchev, Nikita 91
Korolev Sergei 29
Kurchatov, I V 23

Lackman, Flg Off C 138
Laraway, Flt Lt E 69
Ledger, Flt Lt 44
Lee, Godfrey 17

LeMay, Gen Curtis E 30
Lewis, Flt Lt K L 35
Lindsay, Sgt 106
Lippisch, Dr Alexander 17
Lloyd, ACM Sir Hugh P 105-6
Lovett, Wg Cdr K J 145

McDougall, Sqn Ldr C N 138
Mackie, Wg Cdr A C L 65
MacArthur, Flt Lt John 112
McConnell, Maj-Gen John P 106
Macmillan, Harold 117
McNamara, Robert 117

Mallorie, Sqn Ldr Paul 52
Martin-Baker Aircraft Co 20
Masefield, Flt Lt B J 138
Menaul, Gp Capt 44
Millett, Sqn Ldr B T 70
Missiles:
AGM-45A Shrike 136-8
Avro Blue Steel 97-9, 123
Bristol
Bloodhound 86, 119
Type 182 Blue Rapier 97
Convair SM-65 Atlas 48, 87
De Havilland Blue Streak 48-50
Douglas
GAM-87A Skybolt 50, 117
SM-75 Thor 87-91
Goose 87
Lockheed
Polaris 50, 87, 123
Navaho 87
North American
GAM-77 Hound Dog 113-4
Quail 87
R-1 .29
Rascal 87
Redstone Arsenal SM-78 Jupiter 87-8
SA-1 Guild 105
SA-2 Guideline 90
Snark 87
SS-4 Sandal 90
SS-5 Skean 90
V-2 .29
Vickers-Armstrongs
Blue Boar 97
Red Rapier 97

Mitchell, Sqn Ldr P E 33
Monte Bello 33-4, 44
Moyce, W J 33
Myasishchev, Vladimir 24
Nagasaki 9, 23
Nuclear Weapons Tests:
Antler 70
Bravo 46
Buffalo 44
Flagpole 70
Gazette 68
Grapple 68-70
Hurricane 33, 44
Joe 1 23
Joe 2 23
Joe 3 23
Joe 4 45
Koon 46
Mosaic 44, 47
Nectar 46
Romeo 46
Totem 44-5

Yankee 46

Nuclear Weapons/Warheads:
'Little Boy' 9
Blue Danube 21, 33-4, 43-5, 47, 67, 69,
. . . . .70, 87
Green Bamboo 69, 70
Green Granite 69
Indigo Hammer 70, 86
Mk 5 . . . . .93, 123
Mk 7 95
Mk 28 123
Mk 43 123
Orange Herald 70
Pixie 70
Purple Granite 70
Red Beard 70, 123
Red Snow 99
Short Granite 69
Violet Club 87
WE177B 123
Yellow Sun 70, 87, 95, 99

Oakley, Sqn Ldr Rupert 21, 35, 41, 51
O'Connor, Flt Lt S 70
Operations and Exercises:
Black Buck 135-8
Corporate 135
Crossroads 10
Dagger 83
Jungle King 84
Kinsman 103
Mayflight 103
Mick 103
Micky Finn 103
Musketeer 43, 51-6
Rat/Terrier 84
Red Flag 130-2
Oulton, AVM W E 68
Owen, Wg Cdr C B 67

Payne, Sqn Ldr Ronald 75
Penney, Dr William 15
Pierson, Rex 19
Plym, HMS 33-4
Portal, MRAF Lord 15
Prior, Flt Lt Hugh 137
Project E weapons 93-4, 123
Pye, Sqn Ldr Chris 135

Reeve, Sqn Ldr R J 138
Roberts, Sqn Ldr D 35, 43, 70
Robinson, Flt Lt Robert 112
Rowlands, Wg Cdr J S 33
Royal Air Force: Formations and Units:
Bomber Command . . . . .33 et seq
Fighter Command 83-6
No 1 Group 129
No 3 Group 71
No 11 Group 83
No 12 Group 83
No 7 Sqn 119, 150
No 9 Sqn 88, 95, 123, 130, 134, 150
No 10 Sqn 67, 123, 143, 150
No 12 Sqn 95, 119, 123, 150
No 15 Sqn 67, 118-9, 123, 143, 150
No 18 Sqn 109, 119, 150
No 19 Sqn 144
No 24 Sqn 43
No 27 Sqn . . .99, 104, 108, 123, 134, 150
No 35 Sqn 95, 123, 130, 134, 151
No 44 Sqn 95, 123, 129, 135, 15

No 47 Sqn 43
No 49 Sqn 43-4, 49, 68-70, 123, 152
No 50 Sqn 123, 135, 152
No 55 Sqn 119, 123, 144-5, 153
No 57 Sqn . .67, 119, 123, 137, 144-5, 153
No 58 Sqn 69, 70
No 65 (SAM) Sqn 119
No 74 Sqn 144
No 76 Sqn 68-9
No 77 (SM) 89
No 82 SM) Sqn 91
No 83 Sqn . .65, 73, 95, 99, 104, 123, 153
No 90 Sqn 123, 145, 153
No 97 (SM) Sqn 91
No 98 (SM) Sqn 89
No 100 Sqn 68, 99, 100, 153
No 101 Sqn 65, 78, 123, 135
No 102 (SM) Sqn 91
No 104 (SM) Sqn 91
No 106 (SM) Sqn 91
No 107 (SM) Sqn 91
No 113 (SM) Sqn 91
No 130 (SM) Sqn 91
No 138 Sqn 35-7, 41, 51, 119, 153
No 139 Sqn 52-3, 99, 100, 153
No 142 (SM) Sqn 91
No 144 (SM) Sqn 91
No 148 Sqn 43, 51, 123, 148
No 150 (SM) Sqn 91
No 199 Sqn 108-8, 154
No 207 Sqn 43, 51, 123, 154
No 214 Sqn .36, 43, 51, 123, 141, 145, 154
No 216 Sqn 145
No 218 (SM) Sqn 91
No 220 (SM) Sqn 91
No 223 (SM) Sqn 91
No 226 (SM) Sqn 91
No 240 (SM) Sqn 91
No 254 (SM) Sqn 91
No 269 (SM) Sqn 91
No 543 Sqn 37, 43, 106-7, 143, 154
No 617 Sqn 61, 65, 72-3, 77-8, 93, 99,
. . . . .114, 123, 134, 154
No 230 OCU 63, 65, 95, 154
No 232 OCU 37, 67, 154
No 1321 Flt 35, 43, 108
No 1323 Flt 45
Special Duty Flight 105-6
Russell, Flt Lt Richard 137

Sanders, Flt Lt Rex 106
Sandys, Duncan 50, 88, 93
Sheriston, Flt Lt J H 35
Semipalatinsk 23
Shvetsov, A.D. 22
Slater, Flt Lt John 53
Slessor, MRAF Sir John 21
Smallwood, ACM Sir Denis 112
Smeaton, Flt Lt Graham 72
Smith, Flt Lt B 138
Soviet Air Force: Formations and Units
ADD (Soviet Long-Range Aviation) 22
Dal'naya Aviatsiya
(Soviet Strategic Air Force) 22, 27
4th Air Army 27
16th Air Army 27
18th Air Army 22
24th Air Army 27
30th Air Army 27
36th Air Army 27
46th Air Army 27
Spencer, Flg Off 44

Springfields 15
Stacey, Flt Lt 44
Stafford, Reginald S 17
Stalin, Josef 29
Standing, Flt Lt P A 138
Steele, Sqn Ldr A G 70
Streett, Maj Gen St Clair 10
Summers, J. 'Mutt' 21

Taylor, Fg Off Peter 137
Taylor, Flt Lt R E 70
Technical Warfare Committee 14
Tizard, Sir Henry 14
Torlesse, Rear Adml A D 33
Trenchard, Maj Gen Sir Hugh 14
Trent, Wng Cdr L H VC 43, 51
Trevaskus, Flt Lt R 138
Truman, President Harry 9, 23
Tupolev, Andrei 22
Tuxford, Sqn Ldr R 137
Twining, Gen Nathan F 93

United States Air Force
USAFE .30
Air Materiel Command 140
Air Research & Development Command . . .87
Strategic Air Command 10, 30, 37, 87-93,
. . . . .113-7, 140-1
21st Bomber Command 9
7th Air Division 89
2nd BG .30
4th TFW 90
22nd BG 33
28th BG 30-1
43rd BG 11
97th BG 33
301st BG 30-1
307th BG 30, 33
363rd TRW
462nd BW 22
509th BG 10
705th SMW 89
4080th SRW 90
2nd BS .33
19th BS 33
43rd ARS 140
97th ARS 140
91st SRS 140
93rd ARS 141
370th BS 30
371st BS 30
392nd MTS 89
408th BS 33
549th SMS 48
576th SMS 48
771st BS 22
864th SMS 88
865th SMS 88
866th TTS 88

Uranium Commission (USSR) 23

Vinales, Flt Lt J 138

Walker, Sqn Ldr Christopher 112
Washbrook, Flt Lt A 69
Wilson, Charles E 87, 93
Windscale 15
Withers, Flt Lt Martin 137
Woolwich 15
Woomera 44
Wright, Flt Lt R 137